HOSTAGES

A Counter-History of Colonial Plunder

HOSTAGES

A Counter-History of Colonial Plunder

TAINA TERVONEN

Author of *The Bone Whisperers*
Translation by SARA HANABURGH

SCHAFFNER PRESS

Copyright © Éditions Marchialy 2022, Groupe Delcourt
(Original Title—*Les ôtages: une contre-histoire d'un butin colonial*)
Copyright © 2025 by Taina Tervonen
Translation © Copyright 2025 Sara Hanaburgh
All Rights Reserved

This is the first English language edition and first
paperback edition, printed and published by Schaffner Press,
and manufactured in the United States of America.

For permissions and use of excerpts, contact: Permissions Dept.,
Schaffner Press, POB 41567, Tucson, Az 85717.

Cover and interior design by
David Ter-Avanesyan/Ter33Design LLC

Library of Congress Control Number: 2025933353

TABLE OF CONTENTS

Brief Selective Chronology	vi
Prologue	xiii
Ch. 1—To Whom Does Beauty Belong?	17
Ch. 2—"All They Want Are Objects, Not People."	28
Ch. 3—Faidherbe's Hostages	37
Ch. 4—At Second Glance	48
Ch. 5—Caravans and Caravels	58
Ch. 6—The Beginning Of The Story	73
Ch. 7—Two Little Snakes	86
Ch. 8—Archinard's Hostages	98
Ch. 9—The Geopolitics Of Meaning	114
Ch. 10—In The Cave	127
Ch. 11—"All We Were Able To Bring Back Was Abdoulaye"	135
Ch. 12—Objects Of Devotion	145
Ch. 13—The City With No History	159
Ch. 14—The Drum Of Doubt	173
Ch. 15—The Informant	182
Ch. 17—The Little Mute Girl	188
Ch. 18—"Your Grateful and Devoted Abdou Lahi Ahmadou"	208
Ch. 19—The Son of The Vanquished Sultan Ahmadou	219
Ch. 20—To Remain French	226

Ch. 21—"All I Have Are Hypotheses, Nothing Is Certain"	251
Ch. 22—Action Or Truth?	260
Epilogue	273
Acknowledgments	280
Selected Bibliography	282
Author and Translator Biographies	285

SELECTED CHRONOLOGY

Around 1794 Birth of El Hadj Oumar Tall in Halwar.

1821 Creation of the model of the blade of the "saber said to belong to El Hadj Oumar" at Coulaux & Cie, Manufacture Klingenthal, in France

1850 Birth of Louis Archinard in Le Havre.

1864 Death of El Hadj Oumar Tall in Bandiagara.

1879 Birth of Abdoulaye Tall, son of Ahmadou Tall and grandson of El Hadj Oumar Tall

1880 Archinard's arrival in Senegal

1882 First donation of objects to the Ethnographic Museum of the Trocadéro by Archinard

1883 Second donation of objects to the Ethnographic Museum of the Trocadéro by Archinard

1884 Archinard donates two skulls to the Paris Museum of Natural History

1889 Archinard's first donation of objects to the Natural History Museum of Le Havre.

1890 April 6th, siege of Ségou by the French troops led by Archinard. Abdoulaye Tall is captured. Spoils from war—jewelry, manuscripts, various objects—sent to France, as is Abdoulaye.

1891 Archinard's second donation of objects to the Natural History Museum of Le Havre.

1893 February, Permanent Exhibition of the Colonies in Paris. April 29th, siege of Bandiagara by the French troops led by Archinard and defeat of Ahmadou Tall. August 20th, Abdoulaye Tall's first trip to Senegal.

1897 Abdoulaye Tall's second trip to Senegal.

1899 Death of Abdoulaye Tall in Paris at 20 years old.

1909 Archinard donates 69 objects, including "El Hadj Oumar's saber", to the Army Museum.

1914 15 pieces of jewelry are stolen from the "Treasure of Ségou" at the Army Museum.

1929 Archinard's third donation to the Natural History Museum of Le Havre.

1931 Jewelry exhibited at the Colonial Exposition at the Palais de la Porte-Dorée in Paris. The jewelry remained there in storage when the palace took the name the Museum of the Colonies.

1932 Death of Louis Archinard.

1935 The Museum of the Colonies becomes the Museum of France Overseas.

1937 Theft of 45 pieces of jewelry at the Museum of France Overseas (Palais de la Porte Dorée). The Ethnographic Museum of the Trocadéro becomes the Museum of

Man. It also inherits anthropological collections from the National Museum of Natural History.

1960 Senegal achieves independence. The Museum of France Overseas becomes the Museum of Arts from Africa and Oceania.

1993 Thierno Mountaga Tall's mission to Paris to see the manuscripts.

1995 Repatriation of Abdoulaye Tall's remains in Dakar, then inhumation in Ségou.

1998 First loan of the "saber said to belong to El Hadj Oumar" for the bicentenary of the birth of the religious guide, organized in Dakar.

2006 Inauguration of the Quai Branly Museum which inherited collections from the Museum of Arts from Africa and Oceania and the Museum of Man.

2007 The Palais de la Porte-Dorée, built for the Colonial Exposition in 1931 and which then housed the Museum of the Colonies, then the Museum of France Overseas, then the Museum of Arts from Africa and Oceania, becomes the National Museum of Immigration History.

2008 Second loan of the "saber said to belong to El Hadj Oumar" for an exhibition organized at the Théodore-Monod Museum, in Dakar.

2011 Thierno Madani Tall's mission to Le Havre, to see the objects in the city's Natural History Museum. Ephemeral exhibition in the salons of Le Havre's city hall.

2014 Loan of objects of the Museum of Le Havre to the annual Ziarra (pilgrimage) in Dakar.

2018 Third loan of the "saber said to belong to El Hadj Oumar" to the Museum of Black Civilizations which opened in Dakar in December. Various objects from the Natural History Museum of Le Havre are also loaned out for the same occasion.

2019 On November 17th, ceremony of "restitution" of the saber by Édouard Philippe. In reality, it is placed in storage for five years.

2020 On December 24th, the French parliament passes a law which officially restores ownership of the "saber said to belong to El Hadj Oumar" to the Republic of Senegal.

*To archivists throughout the world,
guardians of memory and small papers,
without whom this story could
never have been told.*

PROLOGUE

The caliph Thierno Madani Tall asked me his question in Pulaar. His voice was calm like those who were used to preaching and being listened to. His voice reminded me of my father's, a pastor who at times spoke in a similar tone, which I called his "work voice," when speaking to his children when he wanted to emphasize the seriousness of a particular matter.

Sitting on the edge of a large sofa across from him in this living room where he regularly received the faithful, I fixed my gaze on this Muslim dignitary. Sitting up straight, I waited politely for his question to be translated into French by the friend who had accompanied me here. He told me in advance: "For this first meeting, the caliph will be the one asking the questions, not you." We could hear the noises of the working-class district of the Médina drift in through the open door to the courtyard where the faithful, gathered around large bowls of rice, were finishing their meal. It was early afternoon. Traffic was picking up in the crowded streets of Dakar. A neighbor's sheep were bleating. The interpreter resumed:

"Why are you—a white woman, a descendant of the colonizers—interested in this story?"

The story to which the caliph was alluding was that of his ancestor, El Hadj Oumar Tall, an erudite Muslim and religious and military leader who left northern Senegal in 1850 to wage a holy war. He fought, first, against the French colonizer Faidherbe, then against the Bambara kingdoms, an animist culture, on the land that is present-day Mali. He died "mysteriously" in 1864 in the caves of Bandiagara during a battle that Senegalese children now learn about in their history lessons. His conquests resulted in the birth of the Toucouleur Empire, a Muslim state that his son Ahmadou Tall led until he fell to French troops in Ségou, the empire's capital, on April 6, 1890.

On that day, the French entered Ségou, led by Colonel Louis Archinard, a native of Le Havre and a future general. He found neither Ahmadou nor his men who had fled. To mark their victory, the troops stole a treasure. Weapons, gold and silver jewelry, and 518 manuscripts which belonged to the late El Hadj Oumar Tall. Most importantly, the French Colonel kidnapped the sovereign's son, a child, who was about ten years old. Courageous young Abdoulaye was found in a hut, saber in hand. The pillaged loot, including the saber and the jewelry, was sent to Paris. The child went with it: he was also part of the plunder.

From that moment on, the objects belonged to France. First displayed in exhibits of colonial museums, they were later placed on reserve where they remain to this day, invisible to the public. The situation was so absurd that, for almost thirty years, the caliph and his family had been demanding that their property be returned, but to no avail. What was impeding it? I came to see him so that he could tell me his version of the story.

But for now, the caliph was the one asking the questions. The interview almost fell through, since I was dealing with a very busy man who had other priorities than to explain history to white people like me who after four hundred years of colonial and postcolonial co-existence had proven that listening was not their strong suit. My ancestors were not Gauls; they were Finnish lumberjacks and peasants. I spent my childhood here, on Senegalese school benches on the sandy streets of small towns where my parents were Protestant missionaries. I summarized those first fifteen years of my life for the caliph, after the customary greetings and thank yous.

But my story did not matter. I was white, and the caliph and I both knew that color stuck to one's skin as well as to one's eye. Mine determined my place in history, and I had to live with that.

So began with that.

"Colonization is a history that we have lived through together, white people and black people. Except it is never talked about as a shared history. Neither here, nor there. And just like anything in the past that is not talked about, it ends up creating problems elsewhere, coming up again and again when one least expects it. In this case, it can be useful to go back."

A smile emerged under the caliph's white beard. He understood French but waited for the Pulaar translation. That is how this would go. In his language. Not in the language of the colonizer, whose ghost haunted our exchanges. Imposing, with his wide white robe draped over the sofa, the caliph listened to me, then replied as my friend translated: "He says that you are interesting."

TO WHOM DOES BEAUTY BELONG?

QUAI BRANLY MUSEUM,
PARIS, FRANCE

For me, the story began six months earlier, at the Quai Branly Museum, in Paris. I had come to look for the objects that belonged to El Hadj Oumar Tall, but instead of finding any trace of the story I was looking for, I spent an afternoon in the Africa Hall seated on a bench watching visitors coming and going amongst the works. In front of me, in the middle of the room, were three human-sized statues placed prominently on display on pedestals, considered to be the cornerstones of the collection. They represented three generations of 19th century sovereigns from the Dahomey kingdom—what is today Benin: the Shark-Man for King Béhanzin, the Lion-Man for King Glèlè, and the Bird-Man for King Ghézo. The Shark-Man was looking at me, one fist in the air, the other held out in front of him. It was my first time seeing that statue, but I knew who Béhanzin was. In the dim-lit exhibition hall, the history lessons I learned at primary school in Senegal came back to me, lessons about those who had resisted the French colonizer, and Béhanzin was among the heroes. As were El Hadj Oumar Tall, Lat Dior Ngoné Latyr, Samory Touré—all names that mean nothing here, in France, but whom everyone knows by heart in Senegal.

Perhaps that is why the description of the Shark-Man was so shocking to me. It read: "Gift: General Dodds." Alfred Amédée Dodds is precisely the man who Béhanzin fought, the French general who led the colonial troops into the kingdom's capital, Abomey, and ordered the pillaging of the palace following bloody battles.

As I sat there on the bench, I thought about Dodds commanding his men to go in and save the statues in the palace Béhanzin had left burning so as not to leave anything to the enemies he had been fighting for two years. How he must have wanted those sculptures as tall as a man. And the throne measuring nearly two meters high. And the palace doors, unsealed and transported all the way to Paris where Dodds indeed "donated" them to Quai Branly's ancestor, the Musée de l'Homme (Museum of Mankind).

A group of kindergarten children accompanied by field trip chaperones crossed the room. They all had on yellow vests and lanyards around their necks indicating the name of their school. Their chirping reminded me of a flock of sparrows. They were white, black, Asian—a reflection of Paris's ethnic diversity, an image that had seduced me when I set foot in this city for the first time. This was where my Senegalese history could exist. All I had to do was take the metro and get off at the Château Rouge station in the north of the capital to soak up the ambiance of an African market. Since then, I learned that most French people ignore their colonial past, a history I learned by heart. But they are its inheritors, much more than I am.

A young black woman passing by, alone, stopped in front of Béhanzin's palace doors, photographing them in detail with her telephone, then turned toward the statues for another shot.

A white couple in their thirties followed, lingering in front of the throne.

"Still, when you think we would take all that from them when we can just take the metro to see the Saint-Denis Basilica . . . it's right there. But for them . . ."

"No, we didn't take it from them. It was bought. Or, rather, it was a gift."

"Obviously it was taken!"

No reaction from the Shark-Man. He was waiting. After more than a century in French museums, he was getting ready to return to his homeland. On November 23, 2018, Emmanuel Macron promised Benin that France would return 26 of the 3,157 works that originated from the country, which were listed among Quai Branly's collections, the Shark-Man among them. However, the jewelry stolen from Ségou during the looting of Ahmadou Tall's palace was not on display. It had lain dormant in the museum's reserves for many years, like the other objects of the spoils of war referred to in the inventory as "Archinard's funds." They had been divided as discretionary awards of the colonial administration, then "gifted" by Louis Archinard. El Hadj Oumar Tall's manuscripts—religious texts written in Arabic—are presently held at the France's National Library. The saber that young Abdoulaye brandished to protect his mother is part of the permanent collection at the Army Museum. A drum, some clothing, a horse saddle and other everyday objects ended up at the Museum of Natural History in Le Havre, the birthplace of Colonel Archinard who, in the 1920s, took it upon himself to carefully arrange certain pieces in the display cases.

In Quai Branly's Africa Hall, the only trace I could find of that history was a plaque commenting on a series of figures painted on stones, taken from caves in Bandiagara where El Hadj Oumar Tall had disappeared in 1864. According to the plaque, the stones were a "gift from Lieutenant Luis Desplagne, Dakar-Djibouti Mission." That ethnographic mission, carried out in the early 1930s, resulted in France's acquisition of about 3,500 objects. I browsed the display cases, thinking back to my primary school lessons, and I noticed an odd mise-en-scène of colonial history, transformed into a narrative of gift-giving, completely devoid of any trace of warring violence or domination or any reference to the brutality to which those objects are direct witnesses.

I found the silence deafening.

A few days later, I headed directly to the archives at Quai Branly. In the consultation room, staring at the computer screen, I felt confronted with the same silence. The twenty-four documents in reference to El Hadj Oumar Tall or Ahmadou Tall—including about ten photographs of the objects—said little about the origins of the jewelry and about how they got to Paris. The documented inventory only included a brief physical description: "gold necklace"; "solid silver bracelet;" "leather and gold child's necklace." I recognized shapes in the photos that were familiar to me, shapes that West African jewelers always reproduced.

The oldest document was dated February 4, 1893. It was a reproduction of a single page from the newspaper, *L'Illustration*. Side by side, I saw one article titled "Snowshoe Races," written by "a correspondent from Finland," and another titled "Treasure Trove of Ahmadou, King of Ségou." The coincidence brought a smile to my face. The article described the opening of a "very interesting" exhibition at the Palais de l'Industrie (Palace of Industry), on the premises allocated to the Permanent Exhibition of the Colonies. It was the first time the jewels had been on display for the Parisian public, along with other objects that had been taken in Ségou: "King Ahmadou's tent, earthenware vases or water jugs, and tabalas, types of bass drums that represent Sudanese sacred relics."

The text was cut off; the article was not reproduced in its entirety. Since there was no visual representation of the exhibition, I imagined how the Palace of Industry had been decorated, on the Champs-Élysées, where the Petit and Grand Palais stand today. The tent, the drums, the water jugs and the jewels (were they in the first or the second room, next to the tent or were they presented separately?). Then, three years after the siege of Ségou, Parisian visitors had come to admire the loot from the conquest of Ahmadou's palace. It was the period of colonial expansion, and the permanent Exhibition of the Palace of Industry was its metropolitan showcase.

This phenomenon was not unique to France. Large museums in several European cities opened during those years. The British Museum's "ethnographic galleries" date back to 1881. In 1882, the Trocadéro Palace in Paris became the Museum of Ethnography, the Museum of Man's and the Quai Branly Museum's ancestor. Berlin's was inaugurated in 1884, the year when "the carving of Africa" took place in the German capital, a conference during which European states sliced up the continent's sub-Saharan region like a cake, each taking for themselves pieces whose borders at times seem to be traced with a ruler. If the primary aim of that conference was to establish rules for the game of commerce, the text that came out of it also stipulated that "the missionaries, the scholars, the explorers, their escorts, goods and collections will be [. . .] under special protection." It was the first time that an international diplomatic text referred to the objects as such.

Other museums would follow suit at the turn of the century: the Tervuren museum in Belgium in 1897, the Linden Museum in Stuttgart in 1911, and the Colonial Museum in

Lyon in 1922. They gradually filled up as the colonial expansion carried on. Curators would place their orders with explorers, missionaries or the military.

Nearly seventy percent of the sixty-nine thousand African objects that the Quai Branly Museum holds today came into its collections between 1885 and 1960. Only one thousand are exhibited today. The others, such as the jewelry from Ségou, only exist for the public in the form of inventory photographs, just like those from the archives, which I was looking at on the computer screen.

I stopped at one of the clichés where several pieces of jewelry were marked with a red cross. "Stolen," the manuscript legend indicated. There were forty-six of them in all, mostly gold jewelry, taken by burglars the night of November 16th-17th, 1937, on display in their exhibit cases in France's Overseas Museum inside the Palais de la Porte Dorée. I could not stop thinking about one of the numerous objections that had been formulated against restitution: the African states reclaiming the works would not have the means to protect them from theft and trafficking.

Curiously, in the archives, theft was only mentioned in 1960—twenty-three years later—when then curator of the museum's Muslim arts section, Mrs. Olagnier-Riotot, addressed Bel-Air's Commissioner in Paris's 12th arrondissement. She seemed annoyed: she could not find a single trace of evidence regarding theft from the police investigation in the archives. Further, she explained to the police commissioner,

"Ahmadou's treasure [. . .] does not belong to us and [. . .] we must return it to its rightful owner." A copy of the results of the investigation would be useful to "justify the absence of the objects which we cannot return to their rightful owner," she went on.

The rightful owner in question was the Army Museum. In France, this is the museum where objects brought back by officers of the colonial army generally ended up. And that is how the Army Museum inherited the jewels and other objects from Ségou in 1910, after they were first exhibited at the Permanent Exhibition of the Colonies, then at the World's Fair in 1900. They are listed in the inventory as follows: "Collection: Louis Archinard." Just like Alfred Amédée Dodds and the statue of King Béhanzin, history retained the name of the pillager.

The Army Museum did not look any safer than France's Overseas Museum: jewels were stolen from there too during a burglary in May 1914. According to an article in the *Petit Journal*, it was the second theft the museum had had in one year. It was the same burglar, the text indicated. He seemed to know what he was doing: it was a Saturday, a day when the museum was closed, and he had entered through a window—a single pane was broken. The culprit had equipped himself with a chisel," they told us, and the window was cut with a diamond. The stolen jewels were never found, nor were those stolen in 1937.

When Mrs. Olagnier-Riottot took stock of the collections in 1960, people had been through World War II and the jewels were no longer a priority, especially since their status as spoils of war was no longer relevant in the year when several African states declared their independence.

In fact, the new Museum of African and Oceanian Arts sought to erase any reference to the colonial era, as recalled by another document that I had my eyes on, a "note", dated 1994, "about the Treasure of Ahmadou", which described the jewels' journey through the museums as such: "Some silver objects continued to be exhibited until 1960, while other objects remained on reserve. [...] Madame Noll, curator of the Africa section until 1988, never wanted to exhibit those objects because their origin was too much of a reminder of the colonial period."

Too colonial to turn into art objects—the image made me smile. The jewels reminded me of the rebels, fiercely displaying their origins to onlooking Europeans, who no longer controlled them in 1960. However, the French museums were not looking to return the loot either. In March 1961, in a correspondence about said inventory between the Army Museum and the future National Museum of African and Oceanian Arts, one letter stood out. In a letter to his colleague at the Army Museum, the Director of Museums in France informed him about a loan request. It had come from the General Director of France's Archives and concerned the "King Ahmadou El Hadj Oumar's saber and the rest of his treasure, for an upcoming exhibition in Dakar to celebrate Senegal's independence."

On April 4, 1961, Senegal celebrated its first year of independence without the saber. It seems the letter was left unanswered. As I continued my research, I could not find any trace of a loan dating from that year. It was as if those objects that were "too much of a reminder of the colonial period" had to be definitively hidden from sight, and not only in Europe, but in Africa too.

Later, when I was rummaging through the French press archives on the Internet, searching for texts relating to the very first exhibition in 1893, I found the rest of the article from *L'Illustration*, which gave a detailed and admirable description of certain jewels.

"The ninety-six pieces of jewelry on display are ninety-six masterpieces. Some are very old and certainly do not originate from French Sudan. Some are very characteristically Byzantine, and some are even vaguely Syrian."

Another journalist, Adrien Barbusse, added his analysis, which described the exhibition for *Nature* magazine, with many more details, even mentioning "El Hadj Oumar's saber," on display in the jewel room. Regarding the jewels, he wrote: "A cursory examination is convincing enough [...] that these adornments are not all locally made." For Barbusse, the most elaborate pieces, those that were "worthy of serving as European models," would originally come from India, Syria or Byzantium: "All of it comes from elsewhere via different routes taken by caravans from Fez, Darfur and the Nile valley." According to him, only the most basic jewels could be "from French Sudan".

Thus, in 1893, it was impossible to think that those pieces were African: too delicate, too fine, made with techniques that were too sophisticated to be African. Africa could not produce what journalists, upon seeing the jewels, qualified as "originality" and "artistic sentiment." Almost one hundred thirty years later, their view seemed schizophrenic to me: you had to admire the spoils of war, bear witness to domination over Africa, and all the while tell yourself that such beauty could not possibly have come from Africa.

I exited the archives feeling sad. Those objects could never be seen simply for what they were: artifacts of a culture other than our own, carriers of a history and knowledge that is different. No, they were judged, first, as too beautiful to have come from an elsewhere that had been subjected to domination, and then too colonial to be simply admired—including by those who demanded that they be returned.

"ALL THEY WANT ARE OBJECTS, NOT PEOPLE"

SAINT-LOUIS, SENEGAL, WITH JEWELER MAKHTAR NIANG

Sitting on a small stool next to the white plastic chair he took out for me, Makhar Niang carefully studied each of the photos. I had printed the images from the museum's archives six months earlier—all black and white photographs from 1995 of silver jewelry held by Quai Branly—and I brought them to Senegal where I would spend a few weeks tracking down those objects originally from Ségou.

Makhtar Niang was a jeweler. I stopped in front of the window of his miniscule boutique-workshop in one of Saint-Louis's streets where I had set down my suitcases for part of my trip. I appreciated his reaction when I began to bargain over the price of his rings.

"You know, I never bargain. I weigh the piece of jewelry to know the precise weight of the silver that was used, I add the cost of my work, and that sets the price."

We agreed on a price and, just before leaving, I asked him if I could come back to see him with some photos of antique jewelry.

"Of course. I will also show you some photos. I sell antique jewelry from time to time." I went back the very next day. I found Makhtar in the same spot he had been the day before, sitting on the narrow wooden bench propped up against the grey painted metal door, in front of the yellow façade of his shop, that yellow so characteristic of the island of Saint-Louis and its houses inherited from the colonial period, between the yellow of the sun and the color of a baby chick, faded here and there depending on when they had last been painted. My house, the one where I had lived between the ages of six and nine, was the same color. Since then, it had been repainted brick-red, and I barely recognized it when I passed by. But then I saw the yellow peeking out from beneath a patch of flaking paint, which had peeled off due to the constant humidity of the island that sat in the middle of the river. Everywhere, the facades of the houses were like that, with their layers of the past revealing the colors of each scratch left by the sea spray of the Atlantic. The Guet Ndar district, located on the opposite bank, was crumbling. From the island's roof terraces, you could see the waves capped with white foam sweeping over the sand, which, year after year, eat away at the narrow strip of land that is home to the fisherman's district.

As I walked on the island, I was struck by the walls and their past shades of color. I thought of each hue as a layer of history, a different version of the same story. I could spend hours photographing their details, the color variations that traced borders, as maps do of what no longer exists. The curious look of passers-by kept me from lingering for too long in front of a façade. I was embarrassed by the image I feared I was projecting—yet another Toubab raving on about old buildings, some of which were on the verge of collapse. Yet another Toubab searching for dilapidated colonial romanticism. So, I practically hid while taking my photos, as if I were stealing images from the city and its current inhabitants. Makhtar Niang examined the photos of the jewelry, picking them up one by one, turning them over, looking more closely to observe their details.

"That one is Mauritanian" he says showing me three solid bracelets. "The Moors work with massive silver without welding, just with rivets. Do you see the small beads on this bracelet?"

He was pointing at the piece of jewelry in the middle of the photo, two domed semicircles clasped at the wrist, decorated with embossed beads of different sizes.

"They make a hole, pass the bead through it, then flatten it on the other side, that's how it stays in place. That is Toucouleur. They use the clover pattern a lot."

Makhtar pointed to a close-up photograph of a pendant: "And these massive bracelets are also Toucouleur. There are several of them there," he said, looking over several photos. "These here are anklets, and this one is worn in the hair, to decorate braids. Hold on, I have photos. I'm going to show you."

He took his cell phone out of his pocket, scrolling through dozens of photos until he found the one he was looking for. It was an old photo, in black and white: two women seated on either side of a coffee table covered with a tablecloth, atop it a bouquet of flowers. They were young and made up, the sides of their boubous raised exposing their knees and revealing the geometric patterns of their pagnes. They were wearing babouches on their feet, their ankles adorned with jewelry. I recognized the type of massive bracelets from photos from the Quai Branly Museum.

"In Wolof, it's called làmmu tank," Makhtar said.

I repeated after him to memorize it.

"Who is this in the photo?"

"That's my paternal grandmother, Coumba Waly Guèye, and her friend. I can't remember her name. See? She is wearing the same necklace with silver bells that I have in my display case. It's a pattern that we still make."

"What is the date of this photo?"

"I don't know exactly, but it is old. My grandmother passed away around 1940."

Makhtar picked up the pile of photos again.

"That is also Toucouleur, but that one is Bambara," he said pointing to a detail of the photo of a piece of necklace. They are the ones who use bells in jewelry, like this one."

I listened to him speak as the jewelry, whose inventories

found in the Quai Branly's archives told me nothing more than "silver bracelet," and that jewelry that was at least 130 years old came to life through Makhtar's words.

He stopped at the photo of another necklace and smiled.

"These are old agate beads. Hold on, I'm going to show you."

He got up, rummaged through a drawer behind the plexiglass partition separating his shop from his workshop and came back with a piece of cloth in his hand. Inside was a handful of beads in orange hues—they were round, oval, some elongated others flattened, some small and others larger.

"Usually, we string these to make a necklace. I sometimes mount them as a pendant. It's less expensive for the customer."

He told me that he really liked that jewelry. Sometimes he bought them from antique dealers. Occasionally he had orders from customers who were passionate about them like he was, and they would ask him to make reproductions based on a photo.

"You really are passionate."

"Oh yes, it's my passion!" he replied with a smile as he dove back into the photos. "That one is a box for the Koran or for gris-gris. Generally, it is made of copper, brass or silver. It is worn around the neck, over a boubou. And you see this thick chain, with a twist? In Wolof we call it yaxu jaan, which means 'snake bone' because you can make it twist like a snake."

Makhtar told me that he did not intend to become a jeweler. At first, he worked in rice cultivation, then he became a welder. But when he was 25, he left it all to learn the jewelry trade with his father.

"I can't explain why. Here, we say that if you do not know where you are going, look back to where you come from. I am from a family of jewelers on both sides. My mother is from Gandiole, and my father is from Tiaouane, on the road to Touba, which was a village of jewelers, a Ceddo village at the time."

The Ceddo were warriors of ancient Senegalese kingdoms who resisted the Islamification and Christianization of the region, defending not only the ancient kingdoms but also traditional spiritualities. Today, for many, the term has a negative ring to it, synonymous with infidel.

"At first, learning it was hard," Makhtar recalls.

"You make a piece, show it to your father, and he says: 'It's nice.' Then he sends you to show it to two other jewelers. The first one tells you it's good, but the second crushes it and asks you to start all over again. It's to make you understand that working means accepting having your heart broken. A piece of jewelry that takes time to make in the studio lasts longer for the client."

Makhtar's father was now 92 years old. Every morning, he came and sat on the bench propped up against the shop door.

"It pains me to see that not everyone works the way I was taught in the past," Makhtar went on. "That's the reason people think all jewelers are scammers. I don't want that. Making a fake just brings shame to you and to your family."

He looked for another photo on his telephone: the black and white portrait of a young man was yellowed by the sun and crinkled from wear over the years. Strangely, it looked like Makhtar: same mouth, same nose. It was his paternal grandfather, Coumba's husband, who was also a jeweler. Makhtar shared his first name.

"In our family, we are nine children, but I am the only one who became a jeweler. I have a brother who sells jewelry in Cameroon, but he doesn't make it."

Makhtar too spent a few years in Cameroon as his father also had. He explained that all the jewelers there were Senegalese, and that their knowledge was appreciated. One of his uncles, his father's older brother, also a jeweler, had even traveled to France for a show. "Hold on, I'm going to find the photos."

Makhtar got up again to rummage through his shop, then called me over to see. It was an old wooden table with a neon light and a couple of simple tools—pliers, a hammer and a spade. On the ground was a block of wood. In one corner, a stove made from the bottom of a barrel. Its rudimentary décor contrasted with the fineness of the jewelry on display in his shop window on the other side of the plexiglass.

"Is that where you work?"

"Yes. I have everything I need there. It has always been a jewelry studio. I started here in 1997. This is where I found the photos that I wanted to show to you. I can't find them anymore... They must be at home. But if you come back, I will find them for you."

"Okay, then I'll come back."

Before we said good-bye, I told him everything I knew about the history of the jewelry from Ségou, which was not very much: the siege of the city in 1890, its arrival in France, the first exhibitions, the thefts, and that it was currently on reserve. I said that I was not able to see the pieces because they hadn't been exhibited for the last dozens of years. I thanked him for everything he shared and told him that the jewelry had come to life for me as I listened to him speak with such enthusiasm and passion.

He listened to me, thought for a moment, then said: "They should ask the jewelers here to help. We know them, those pieces of jewelry. We would know how to restore them and take care of them."

He was right. I hesitated a little, then decided to tell him that when the jewelry was first exhibited in Paris, journalists did not believe that it could have come from Africa. They considered the pieces too refined to have been made by Africans. Makhtar Niang smiled in embarrassment and raised his eyebrows. I suddenly felt terribly ashamed of my colleagues who had lived one hundred thirty years ago.

Later, when I went back to see Makhtar, he was waiting for me with the photos that he found. There were five of them, 6 x 8 inches in size, printed like large black and white postcards, with the inscription "International Exhibition of Decorative Arts—Paris, 1925." In them we found the "Africa Pavilion," with exterior and interior views of the "native village," with men, women and children posing in traditional outfits under an awning behind jewelry display cases. "Group of artisans selling objects made in their native village," the caption read. Makhtar looked at the photos with me.

"My uncle had gone over there," he said. At the time, that's how it was. They had people go to show what they knew how to do. Nowadays, all they want are objects, not people. The Europeans want to be able to come here, but they do not accept the inverse. They're so afraid that we'll stay."

FAIDHERBE'S HOSTAGES

SAINT-LOUIS, SENEGAL, EL HADJ OUMAR FOUTIYOU TALL HIGH SCHOOL

Mr. Diop, Assistant Principal of El Hadj Oumar Foutiyou Tall High School in Saint-Louis, looked me straight in the eye. He was baffled.

"But . . . tell me, what is the problem with the veil?" He regularly followed French news and the recent debate about the possible ban on veiled mothers accompanying their children on school trips left him in utter shock.

I ended up in his office when I was looking for the principal's. "She stepped out, but will be back in a moment," the Assistant Principal told me after letting her know that I had arrived. For my part, I hadn't informed anyone that I would be coming. I showed up at the high school unexpectedly, explaining to the main office that I was working on objects that had belonged to the religious leader after whom the school was named. I had heard that the high school would be celebrating its one-hundred-year anniversary the following day and I was hoping to visit the grounds. I was directed to the administration wing where I ran into the assistant principal who welcomed me in his office as I waited for the principal.

"The problem isn't so much the veil," I said. Islam is what upsets people, especially since the 2015 terrorist attacks. But it's easier to talk about the veil, rather than talking frankly about the place of Islam in France."

"I really don't understand it," the assistant principal replied shaking his head. "Islam is a religion of peace and forgiveness! Islam is not about cutting off thieves' hands and stoning adulterers. And we suffer from jihadism here in Africa too. But all that has nothing to do with the veil."

I fully agreed with him. The French tension around certain religious symbols seemed incomprehensible in a country where religion was part of daily life, where the calls to prayer rang out several times a day and where on Fridays the lunch break was longer to allow everyone to participate in the afternoon prayer at 2 o'clock. I grew up with the muezzin providing a rhythm to my days, serving as a clock, and a calendar that took into account the Muslim holidays as it did the Christian holidays.

A student knocked at the door, interrupting our discussion. The vice principal listened as she explained her concern, promised to take care of it, and sent her back to class. Then he turned toward me.

"Have you seen the construction of the new square, just next door?"

"Yes, I have seen it. I tried to see the statue of Faidherbe that used to stand in the center of the square, but all I found was a fenced off construction site." Later, I learned that the statue of the former governor of Senegal had been removed during the construction and was unlikely to return. Commemorating Faidherbe, who was known as the "peacemaker" of the colony during his mandate—from 1854 to 1861, then from 1863 to 1864, has been controversial for years. The "pacification" was actually quite bloody as evidenced by the villages that were burned down and the massacres of civilians. But on the pedestal of the statue, erected in 1886, showing the governor standing, a kepi in one hand and a sword in the other, read the message: "To its governor, Louis Faidherbe, Senegal is grateful." An inscription that sounded like an insult to the ears of many in Senegal, which had been independent for sixty years. Yet, for centuries, and despite a controversy that began in the 1970s under the pen of writer and filmmaker Ousmane Sembène, the statue had not moved.

Then, one windy night in September 2017, Faidherbe was brought down by bad weather. We saw images of scenes of jubilation circulating, youth were posing next to the statue on the ground, stepping on his bronze face. That night, the city was filled with followers of Cheikh Ahmadou Bamba, another 19th century resistance fighter, a religious leader like El Hadj Oumar Tall, and founder of the Mouride brotherhood. His followers had gathered in Saint-Louis to celebrate "the day of the two rakaas," as they did each year, which commemorated the departure into exile of their leader, captured and judged by the colonizer in the neighboring governor's palace in 1895. True, Cheikh Ahmadou Bamba and Faidherbe never actually confronted one another, the latter having been dead and buried for six years at the time when the former was captured, but still. A rumor had spread throughout the city: perhaps the wind was not solely responsible for the statue falling. Perhaps the storm had been aided by a few arms determined to take down the symbol of colonialism.

What was certain, it was concluded, was that even the Cheikh had approved of the fallen statue. Such a coincidence regarding dates could not be anything other than a divine message. Religion informed everything here, the debates about memory.

"Seems like they're going to put free Wi-Fi in the square," the assistant principal went on. "That's going to be a big problem. Can you imagine what that means for us?"

He opened one of his desk drawers and took out five cell phones.

"See this? I confiscate them for seventy-two hours when the students used them in class. Then I call their parents to let them know. But some of them don't even answer when I call! People truly have no manners today."

His weariness made me smile. So, in Saint-Louis and in Paris, the vice principals and school monitors were fighting the same battle against the dark forces of the screen, an everyday battle against that fetish hidden in youths' pockets that bewitched the brain.

When I joined the principal in her office at the other end of the hall, two other people were already there: a woman my age, in her forties, and an older man with a white beard and a mischievous air. The principal introduced them to me: they were the daughter and the cousin of a former principal of the high school, the late Abou Touré. During the centenary celebration which would take place the next day, the teachers' room was to be renamed in his memory with a plaque bearing his name.

"And what about you? What brings you here today?" asked Arête Sarr Mbodj, the principal, turning toward me.

I explained my project again: the objects from Ségou, their traces, the high school's name. Abdou Touré's daughter, whose name I later learned was Ndiabou Séga Touré, was looking at me with a mix of interest and surprise.

"So, I wanted to know if it would be possible for me to attend the party and perhaps take a few photos of the event," I added.

"Of course, no problem. We were just discussing how the day would go in fact. Mr. Kane was telling us what he remembers about the establishment. He was in the same graduating class as Abou Touré, who was first a student at the high school, and then went on to become a teacher and later a principal."

"The class of 1946!" the old man specified with a smile. "We were 200 students—Lebanese, French, Senegalese, Malians, Guineans, there were even two students from Dahomey."

He did not say Benin. Instead, he said Dahomey, the name that part of Africa had during the colonial period. Similarly, instead of saying "El Hadj Oumar Foutiyou Tall High School," he said "Faidherbe High School," the name the establishment had borne since its creation in 1919 until 1984 when the Minister of Education decided to rename several schools. I too knew the high school as Faidherbe when I lived in Saint-Louis in the early 1980s. It was a top-notch high school that assembled the best students in Senegal, some who came from Casamance at the other end of the country. I smiled back at Mr. Kane, obviously very proud of having been among those in the school's first class, which brought together the best students, not only from Senegal but also from all of French West Africa.

"It is courageous of you to tackle this story about El Hadj Oumar Tall," his niece suddenly said to me, "It's a sensitive topic."

I could hear the caution in her voice, even though for the time being I had no idea what eggshells I was about to walk on. I had to remember to be guided, I told myself.

Two days earlier, I read the speeches that were given at the high school's very first "patron celebration" on April 27, 1985, on the first anniversary of that new name, which Mr. Kane was unable to accept as his own. I had opened the door to the Center for Research and Documentation in Saint-Louis, located on the southern tip of the island, its windows open to the river that flowed towards the ocean. Outside, a herd of goats bleated as they trotted down the street. There were onlookers sitting on the low wall lining the sidewalk, watching a film crew getting ready for a shoot of a TV series in front of the building turned town-hall. "Action!" Inside the library classroom, a teacher was explaining the concepts of material and immaterial heritage in French and in Wolof to a small group of middle schoolers. "Is Gorée's House of Slaves material or immaterial heritage? And what about ceebu jënn?" I thought about Ségou's treasure: material heritage. Very much so.

I opened the first folder the archivist brought me. It was bright orange with thin yellowed pages inside. In his speech, one of the high school's history and geography teachers told the story of El Hadj Oumar Tall's life from his birth in Halwar in northern Senegal "between 1794 and 1797" up to the jihad that started in 1850 with the conquest of the Soninke and Bambara animist kingdoms in what is present-day Mali—including the kingdom of Ségou, which was taken in 1860 and given to his son Ahmadou, then continued with the conquest of the Muslim kingdom of Macina even further to the east.

In the same folder was another speech, given by Thierno Mountaga Tall, caliph of the Tijani, one of the great Senegalese brotherhoods with the Mourides. The speech, described as the "original translation, faithful to the official Arabic text, was addressed to the Minister of Education:

The decision of the Senegalese government to name this high school, the country's oldest secondary school, after the hero and fighter Cheikh El Hadj Oumar Tall al Foutiyou, although it bore the name of one of his fiercest adversaries, namely Faidherbe, takes on a deep and powerful meaning. We thank Allah for guiding the government to this choice, which has allowed us to replace it with the name El Hadj Oumar, who fought for Faith and against colonialism, against the colonizer, the usurper and oppressor that Faidherbe was.

"Faidherbe supporters will always be Faidherbe supporters!" Mr. Kane explained in the principal's office. He had no intention of becoming an Oumar supporter.

"The elders are so attached to that name, the principal laughs. I've even gotten into the habit of saying: El Hadj Oumar Foutiyou Tall—formerly Faidherbe—High School!"

I had the impression that had nothing to do with admiration for the historic figure, but rather with the nostalgia the elders had for their golden youth.

My impression was confirmed the following day when I returned for the party. In the high school courtyard, the first rows of seats were occupied by the guests of honor, most of them former students, well-dressed, wearing Bazin boubous or suits; there were legislative members, lawyers, doctors and professors, important people referring to the good old days, the greatness of days gone by, restoring values.

Then Abou Touré's daughter, Ndiabou Séga Touré, began speaking. She addressed the students: "My father was of the generation that always fought. He fought for independence in the student movements. He fought in the unions. He fought for education. So, I invite you to reflect on your traditional education, which is increasingly being lost. It is up to you to choose what your tradition consists of, and what so-called 'modern' civilization consists of and to connect them in your own way, so that we can move forward. If you do not know where you come from, it is difficult for you to know where you are headed."

As I listened to her, I thought about Faidherbe's story with the schools in Saint-Louis, a story that began long before the creation of this high school in 1919. It began in 1855 and its objective was something entirely different from "knowing where we come from in order to know where we are headed."

That was the year that Faidherbe established, initially on a trial basis, the "School for Hostages." The name denoted the establishment's aims quite clearly: to welcome the sons of chiefs, subjects of colonial power, who were designated by the governor and sent there to receive a French education. They would then become interpreters in the service of the colonial administration, intermediaries between the two worlds, cut off from the former without fully belonging to the latter. The school institutionalized the already existing practice of kidnapping the sons of chiefs to keep them under their control.

In 1864, Faidherbe renamed the establishment the "School for Sons of Chiefs and Interpreters," a less controversial name for an objective that remained unchanged. Turning heirs to the throne into faithful servants of colonial power was also the intended plan for Abdoulaye, El Hadj Oumar Tall's grandson, about ten years old, who was taken from Ségou along with the jewels, the manuscripts and the saber that the boy had in his hand to defend his mother.

When Abdoulaye was taken hostage by Archinard in 1890, the School for Sons of Chiefs and Interpreters in Saint-Louis still existed, even though Faidherbe was no longer there. The colonial school system was even supplemented by other schools set up along the Senegal River and on the French Sudan side (present-day Mali), always for the same purposes. So, why was Abdoulaye sent to France and not to one of those colonial schools? To make him completely forget "where he came from?"

As I listened to Ndiabou Séga Touré, I thought about that contradiction, with which I was also familiar: the language of the former colonizer was still the one that was taught. It was still the language of knowledge and of administration. It was the language in which I had learned the history of those who resisted colonization, the very people who fought against imposing that language and the culture that goes with it.

Later, I would go to see what the School for Sons of Chiefs and Interpreters was. The building to which the school was transferred in 1902 was still standing, toward the Sor market, on the mainland side of the city. The façade was decorated with earthenware brought from France. The courtyard was square and shaded by the leaves of a large kapok tree, surrounded by yellow and pale pink walls, the Director's office on the ground floor, blue doors along the corridors of its two stories. The building subsequently housed the Ameth Fall Girls' High School, and after that, the Khayar Mbengue Primary School. Now deserted, falling into ruin in some places, it had the sad beauty of abandoned places—notebooks littering the floor of a classroom, debris from a section of the ceiling that collapsed, a lesson still written on the chalkboard: "Tuesday, November 21, 2012."

In front of the entrance gate, a sign recalled the history of the building. On it was a reproduction of an engraving: five teenagers sitting cross-legged on the floor, an adult male sitting behind them. The caption read: "Yoro Diaw, son of Chief Fara Penda of Walo; Demba, son of King Sambala of Medina; Ousman, hostage guard."

AT SECOND GLANCE

SAINT-LOUIS, SENEGAL CENTER FOR RESEARCH AND DOCUMENTATION

The following week, I was back at the Center for Research and Documentation, on the southern tip of the island.

I spent several days boning up on *The Pioneers of Sudan, before, with, and after Louis Archinard* by Jacques Méniaud. The author's description indicates that the book was essentially dedicated to Louis Archinard's glory: "Average height, slender build, broad shoulders, fine features and the perfect regularity of his face, chestnut hair and mustache, with golden-brown slightly myopic eyes peering through his pince-nez." More specifically: "One of the striking features of Archinard's character was his kindness." That is what was said.

Louis Archinard arrived in Senegal in October 1880. Faidherbe no longer ruled Saint-Louis, or the colony, but he did control the city, which the officer learned had become the former governor's project: the island with its gridded streets, its governor's palace and cathedral, and the native districts relegated to the periphery, separated from the administrative center by the river.

Archinard did not stay long in Saint-Louis. He left swiftly for Kayes, in what is today Mali. He needed to lead the French troops there to secure the building site whose budget the French Parliament had just passed: a railroad was to be built connecting Senegal's Atlantic coast to the French Sudan's interior to transport merchandise and men. To save money, it was decided that the first portion of this new route would be by water, on the Senegal River from Saint-Louis to Kayes, then the railway would take over all the way to Bafoulabé.

The trip began badly. Men had fallen sick since they left Saint-Louis, the river was full of grass that had to be cut to allow the boat to pass through, a third of the troops immediately came down with malaria, typhoid or sunstroke. In Archinard's letters to his brother Frédéric, he recounted the setbacks which nevertheless did not seem to wear him down.

November 23, 1880.

My last letter was dated the 17th, when we were about to disembark from the Éclair in Tamboukaré. That disembarkation was still very arduous. I was misled about the means of transport, and we barely had any food left. Personally, I do not care much for those things. I like couscous and, with it, a piece of *meat and some water. I think we make a fine dinner, you know, it's a bit like our beefsteak and rice, but it's not the same thing for the troops.*

Once they had arrived, Archinard noticed that the work was not progressing at all as planned. During the first "campaign," from 1881 to 1882, only a little over half a mile had been built. The French sent Moroccans and Chinese to help at the construction site, but that did not go well. Fights broke out, and the Chinese were "poorly regarded by the Blacks." Archinard was tired, came down with a fever, a tapeworm, and a "hordeolum" on his eye, but continued to write letters to his brother and to his friends recounting his days as a colonist, about which he said he had no complaints: "On the whole, all is well."

Kita, February 16, 1881.

For my birthday on February 11th, I had a fine military celebration this year. We had to fight to take Goubanko. Now, I believe they will leave us peacefully to our work.

Kita, February 28, 1881.

The copper bracelets that I brought from France have been very successful for obtaining food. The other day, I exchanged them for a goat. The Blacks who had sold it to us were so happy that they left gesticulating and dancing: they must have lost the bracelet on the way because I found it the following day, in the grass not far from our camp. There's a goat that did not cost me much.

Bamako, February 16, 1883.
We have had some nice lunches on the banks of the Niger, and we often have excellent fish. Our cook recently made us an impossible dish that he calls chicken goat skin. He had removed the skin from a chicken and attached its legs, wings and neck to make a sort of sack that he had sewn up after stuffing it with bits of fish, so that we were served a plump chicken which looked very good, and when we cut it up, we found a fish dish. Not great, I must admit.

Bamako, April 24, 1883.
I no longer have any underclothes. Fortunately, I have left some in Kita, in Kayes and in Matam, which I will pick up on my way back.

Badumbé, December 26, 1883.
My horse has died.

By that date, the rails had been laid up to mile 10.5 and the bush cleared up to mile 23.5. It had been three years since the work had begun.

I looked up from the book in a daze after dozens of pages of detailed descriptions glorifying Archinard. Through the window, I saw some high school girls in their physical education class running two by two along the river, some lagging behind preferring to chatter among themselves. You could tell who they were by their pink t-shirts bearing the name of their institution: Ameth Fall High School, heir to the former School for Hostages. In 1965, the high school was relocated to a building that used to be a hospital, adjoined to the Research Center.

The name of the school is not insignificant. Ameth Fall was neither a resistance fighter nor a spiritual guide like El Hadj Oumar Tall. He was a hostage guard. The sons of chiefs who had been kidnapped before Faidherbe's school opened were entrusted to him. He subsequently became the school's Dean of Discipline.

As I watched the young girls running along the river, I wondered who had taken them hostage one hundred sixty-five years after their "patron" had taken the job. Why hadn't this high school been renamed in the 1980s, like the former Faidherbe High School? Was it because Ameth Fall was Senegalese? Perhaps that was symbolic enough despite his position in the colonial administration.

I had a feeling that everything in that city was like that: a mixture of traces from the past that were at once criticized and celebrated, renounced and glorified, where it would have been impossible for a foreigner to discern the logic. In order to grasp some of the nuances, you had to delve into the history of the city, go back four hundred years through its shared history with the French, to 1638. That was the year the Rozée Company from Dieppe opened a trading post in Saint-Louis, after Richelieu had granted him a trade monopoly over Senegal and the Gambia—more precisely: Norman sailors were navigating along the West African coasts as early as the second half of the 14th century looking for ivory. The city's name was a tribute to Louis XIV, which in no way prevented its Wolof name, Ndar, from continuing to exist. Moreover, the people from Saint-Louis still refer to themselves as doomi Ndar, the children of Ndar.

The first relationships between the French and the doomi Ndar were thus established through trade: first, in leather and Arabic gum, then the Atlantic slave trade to supply the sugar plantations in the West Indies. The slave trade was carried out in the 17th and 18th centuries by the French West India Company, then by the Senegal Company, which soon faced competition from traders from the ports of Bordeaux, Nantes and Saint-Malo.

The traders had their say in colonial policy, including after the ban on slavery. In the 1850s, it was their influence that made Faidherbe governor. One of the merchants from Saint-Louis, Hubert Maurel of Bordeaux, brought his personal friendships to bear on the government so that the modest captain he had met at Saint-Louis would be named commander, then governor of the colony in 1855. The pact was clear: to methodically reinforce the colonial apparatus and "pacify" the territory to allow trade to prosper. Hubert Maurel and his cousin and associate Hilaire Prom, who had arrived in Senegal thirty years earlier, had a plan: to make a fortune from peanut oil, at the time unknown in Europe. To do that, they intended to develop large-scale cultivation of the seed in the colony. Faidherbe would uphold his part of the agreement. His bloody conquests of several Senegalese kingdoms would benefit Maurel & Prom's business, which two years after the new governor's nomination would open the Bacalan Oil mill in Bordeaux, followed by two other oil mills in Marseille, and new trading posts in Senegal. The Bordeaux location still exists. It was since named Lesieur Alimentaire and Céréol. As for Maurel & Prom, that company now specializes in the extraction of oil and natural gas, particularly in Gabon and Tanzania.

From those centuries of trade, coexistence and conflicts, a mixed colonial society would be born in Saint-Louis where white men had children with black women in the context of "taking native wives"—children who would subsequently make up the city's elite. The mixed-race women from Saint-Louis, known as "signares," would become influential figures in the city, often prosperous businesswomen, or owners of domestic slaves. Even today, during some of the city's traditional festivals, you can see ladies parading around dressed as signares in long, puffy dresses and pointed headdresses.

The mixed-race elite was an integral part of colonial society. They served in the colonial administration and the army, just like the white French people who came from France. A descendant of that same mixed-race elite was Alfred Amédée Dodds, born in Saint-Louis in 1842, the same man who ordered the sacking of Béhanzin's Royal Palace and had the statues of the Shark-Man, the Bird-Man, the Lion-Man transported to Paris. His paternal grandfather was English, John Dodds, aide-de-camp of the last English governor of Saint-Louis during the brief British occupation which lasted from 1758 to 1779. His ancestor had married a young woman from the city, Sophie Feuilletaine, she herself the daughter of a merchant from Lorraine and a Fulani woman. As for Alfred Amédée's mother, she was the daughter of a French man from Grenada and a Senegalese woman. Young Alfred Amédée Dodds joined Saint-Cyr, enlisted in the colonial troops in Indochina as well as in Senegal, then became senior commander of the French troops in Dahomey.

That was how the city was when Archinard arrived in Saint-Louis in 1880: a mixed-race colonial town where merchants had sustained the military conquests of the surrounding territories. His mission was to expand the territory by thousands of miles, and to develop the secure transport of goods from the Atlantic coast to the interior. It was because of that mission that he deemed it necessary to attack Ségou, where he would steal jewelry, the saber and manuscripts, and find himself face to face with young Abdoulaye.

The former Maurel & Prom building still stands in Saint-Louis. The building has been abandoned, like so many others. A man opened the door for me. He sat down in a large dark room on the ground floor with a low ceiling and paint flaking off the walls in hues of blue, white and gray. He said he was an artist who worked with fish skins.

After some negotiation, he allowed me to tour the building that was falling into ruin. In the courtyard, the double staircase leading to the upper floors had partly collapsed, its steps covered in vegetation. On the second level, vast empty rooms were plunged into darkness, the floor covered in dust. On the third level, a veranda and other brighter rooms sat beneath an attic roof. Like everywhere in that city, the walls were covered in several layers of successively colored paint. In one spot was a white wall, a rectangle where golden yellow, sky blue and khaki green blended together with a few touches of burgundy and navy here and there.

I thought about those two cousins who had set out from Bordeaux on an adventure at the beginning of the 19th century, the first only fifteen years old, the second joining him a few years later, at the age of twenty-two. The colony was full of possibilities: to make money and succeed, even if it meant dreaming a little. How were they so different from the Senegalese youth today who venture out onto the sea heading towards Europe?

When I went back down to the courtyard, the same dweller called me over-eager to show me other rooms on the ground floor, which were cramped, with red brick walls, the only opening a tiny skylight flush with the ceiling. "These were the slave quarters," he said. Later, while looking for information in an inventory of the island's buildings, I learned that Maurel & Prom had purchased all the buildings one by one on this block. The slave quarters dated from the 18th century.

Nowadays, Saint-Louis hardly boasts about its history in the slave trade. Gorée Island, off the coast of Dakar, is now recognized as an historical site, even beyond the country's borders. Gorée is a tourist destination where Afro-descendants of the victims of the Atlantic slave trade go to reflect on the fate of their presumed ancestors—not Saint-Louis, even though several of that island's buildings housed slave quarters. Those same buildings, like all the island's colonial architecture, were classified as cultural heritage by UNESCO in 2000. The city's tourist attraction is this: the decrepit charm of the chick yellow and brick red houses, their wooden shutters and wrought iron balconies. That is what I was also looking at as I photographed the details of the walls on the sly.

Saint-Louis is all those things at once: a city where tradition implores the visitor to go and greet Faidherbe until his statue falls, a city where tourists photograph former slave quarters while ignoring history, a city where a high school still bears the name of a hostage guard. It's as if each and every detail of history were at once a stigma to be rejected and a treasure to be cherished. Perhaps those two truths even existed at first glance.

CARAVANS AND CARAVELS

PODOR, SENEGAL, FORT FAIDHERBE

Ibrahima Sy met me in front of the tall wooden gate of Fort Faidherbe in Podor. I was there to follow the path the French troops had taken in El Hadj Oumar Tall's time, the path they took to conquer Fouta and follow the Senegal River to present-day Mali. I was waiting in the shadow of the enclosure wall, its paint peeling like in Saint-Louis, sheltered from the sun, accompanied by two goats who were rummaging through a pile of trash looking for something to eat, when I saw the old man arrive on my left, leaning on his cane, wearing a small traditional woolen cap, the Cabral cap, sunglasses propped up on it, with a bunch of keys in his hands. He greeted me and opened the gate to the small, shaded garden that we walked across together, up to the three steps that led to the terrace. He looked again for a key, pushed the door and after opening the shutters halfway to let the morning light creep into the room on the ground floor, he invited me to take a seat on a chair, pulled up another one to sit in facing me, and started telling me his story.

"Welcome to Podor's Fort Faidherbe. As we say in Fouta, Podor is a meeting place for the Moors of the desert and the sedentary people of the region. As early as 1744, French traders built a trading port here, later occupied by the English from 1758 to 1783. When the English left, the fort was left abandoned for many years. In the 19th century, the French came back, this time with a very specific goal: to launch their colonial occupation. That was how on March 17, 1854, they took Podor, and Faidherbe had the fort rebuilt in forty days, with two thousand five hundred men: one thousand five hundred French and a thousand Africans."

The sun's rays filtered through the half-open shutters. It was not too hot at that hour, but before long, the heat would beat down on the city like a hammer on the pavement, scorching your scalp and silencing the birds. For the time being, they were still chirping in the garden. I heard them when Ibrahima Sy paused his story. He told me his story the way stories are told here—learned and recited by heart, but always with an element of playfulness: varying the tone, manipulating silence, creating suspense.

"This," Ibrahimy Sy continued, pointing to the room with its pink walls in a sweeping gesture, "is the treasurer's office. The safe that you see there dates to 1854, when the fort was rebuilt. On the ground floor, you also have the officers' office and the soldiers' meeting room. Faidherbe's living quarters are on the second floor. I'll show you later."

The safe was built into the wall, next to the window. Outside, the birds were chirping more intensely.

"The fort was occupied by the French army until 1960, then by the Senegalese army from 1960 to 1984, and after that by the military police until 1997. The fort has been abandoned since the military police left. The people began to loot it: a door one day, a window the next. So, I went to see the mayor. I informed him about it and asked him if I could watch over the place on a voluntary basis. That is how I became the fort's guard. It was just me the first year, in 1997. Then, the second year, there were two of us. We circulated petitions to save the fort. In the end, the French embassy agreed to restore it. It was inaugurated in 2006. At that time, the minister appointed a curator for five years, but there was no operating budget. Now there is someone else, but we always make do with what we have."

He stopped, almost at the end of his story.

"And now it's been twenty-four years that I've been guarding the fort on a voluntary basis. When I am not there, I leave my number on the door. Anyone who wants to visit can call me and I'll come, anytime. You have to respect people who come from far and wide to see this historic monument."

I listened in silence as Ibrahima Sy spoke, as I was taught to do here: never interrupt an adult who is speaking and, most importantly, never interrupt a story. Allow it to unfold according to the narrator's mood, whether they are hurried or taking their time. Whatever the case, listen patiently until the end. I thanked him and asked him how old he was now.

"I'm seventy-four. I worked in agriculture, but I am slightly visually impaired. The children have taken over for me."

"Did you grow up in Podor?"

"Yes, I was born here. I grew up here. Despite the heat, I rarely leave Podor. When I go to Dakar, I don't stay more than a week. The heat caresses my skin."

I watched his hand as it grazed his forearm. It was leathery from the sun and years of work. I smiled as I looked at it. The heat has not been as kind to me.

"Why did you get involved like that with the fort?"

"As I said, it's an historical monument in Podor. And I am connected to Podor. As a child, I went to school next door, with little French kids. I played with them in the fort. That's how I came to love this place."

"What years were you in school?"

"In the 1950s, before independence. We were taught the French education system, with French teachers. I lived through both eras: colonization and independence."

"And what is your takeaway?"

"My takeaway is simple. I say: if you asked me, today, to extend colonization, I would be for it. Back then, there was less corruption, less impunity."

"But the French exerted domination..."

"Indeed. There was colonial domination."

"But everyday life was better?"

"Oh yes! Before, with just twenty-five CFA, we could make tea—the three rounds—for eight or nine people. Now, you need at least three hundred CFA."

I recognized that nostalgia for better, bygone times: a young man gazing at the horizon to imagine a brighter tomorrow, while his elders cherished the memory of what was no more. As we walked up to the second floor, Ibrahima Sy explained that he was looking for someone to ensure his succession. He was getting old, and his eyes were playing tricks on him.

"And, have you found anyone?"

"Not yet. People say you need to move on. But history is not like that. History is what people have lived, what they relate to. You cannot minimize that."

The wooden staircase creaked beneath our feet, the rhythmic thumping of the guard's cane setting the pace of our steps. When we reached the walkway at the top, the sun made us squint. I moved closer to the railing. Before us lay a small garden, enclosed by the outer wall of the fort. Further on the right, the annex, which had been turned into a hotel and a little beyond that, just behind the trees blocking our view was the Senegal River, flowing calmly toward the sea that I had left two days earlier when I had turned my back to the Atlantic Ocean spray to penetrate Fouta's heat. For over a hundred miles, between Saint-Louis and Podor, I had watched the landscape change color, from the dark grey urban asphalt to the green of the sugar cane fields as we approached Richard-Toll and its sugar factory. Beyond Richard-Toll, the horizon became flat and yellow like straw, with no other relief than the thorny shrubs standing as tall as a child, sprouting from the earth here and there, and a few villages of round huts with thatched roofs. Sometimes you would see a boxlike building made of concrete blocks with a slightly leaning tin roof, and a tiny window at the back, houses that looked like small cubes sitting on the sand. As we approached Ndioum, the landscape began to undulate, its dry trees hugging the sides of dunes atop of which a herd of cows was heading toward the river. On the other side of the road, a long, majestic column of them swayed along slowly, the calves clinging tightly to their mothers' hind legs, the latter's large semicircular horns resembling a crown above their gentle gaze. For a little over a hundred miles, the river, to my left, had remained invisible, hinted at simply by the herd's movement and the sprouting green despite the dry season. Then, as I left National Route 2 after Tarédji, at the fork in the road toward Podor, its presence became increasingly obvious in the vast green fields along its banks, in the dry bed of an arm awaiting wintering, to impose itself at my arrival on the quay, an unphased current half-green, half-indigo depending on the light and angle. On the other side was Mauritania.

"This was Faidherbe's office."

I turned toward Ibrahima Sy. He was opening the corridor doors one by one.

"This was his dining room, and over there was his office."

I accompanied him into the different rooms, which became bathed in light as he opened the shutters, the sun exposing our footprints left on the dusty ground.

In the office was a desk, a table, one chair, a horse saddle laying on the floor, and a rifle propped against the wall. There was also a gridded map of the city, titled "Building project for 1861-1862" indicating the fort and merchants' houses along the quay, exactly where they currently sat, although those buildings had been repurposed, one as an inn, another a school; others were left abandoned. The fort was intended to protect French trade, primarily that of rubber arriving from Mauritania, which, up to that point, had been subject to various taxes and customs paid to the local chiefs. When they took possession of Podor and rebuilt the fort, France had also decreed that the Senegal River belonged to them and, thus, there was no longer any need to pay those taxes. The merchants settled along the quay, which was equipped for large boats coming from Saint-Louis, whose keels provided the stability they needed to traverse the Atlantic, but also prevented them from going further upriver.

I walked through each of the rooms. In the dining room was a table with four chairs, a hutch above which hung a portrait of Napoléon III. The bedroom had one metal bed and a trunk. The sounds of the city drifted in through the open windows: children from the neighboring school, the call of the muezzin. In the garden below, lethargic from the heat, the birds became quieter. As I ambled along, I could hear Ibrahima Sy's cane as he entered the hallway. He paced up and down, then stopped. Through the open door, I could see his slender silhouette leaning against the corridor windowsill, his gaze turned toward the invisible river behind the trees.

Later that afternoon, when the sun became softer, I set out to find the home of Abdourahmane Niang, who was the first to guard the fort and a friend of Ibrahima Sy. "He is sort of my teacher," the latter said as he gave me directions: "it's the house on the corner, next to School 1." A young girl opened the door and asked me to wait a moment so she could see if Abdourahmane Niang was available to receive me. He was an older man. It was the middle of the month of Ramadan, and I had knocked at his door unannounced, despite having thought it better not to disturb him.

"It's OK, come in," the young girl called out to me.

Upstairs, I found an old man with a white beard sitting on a mat with a prayer rug next to him.

"Sit down!"

I sat in the armchair facing him, and we exchanged the customary greetings: How are things in France? And your family here? And how is fasting going, not too hard with the heat? That was what was always done. Whether you and your interlocuter knew each other or not, you always took the time to sit down and greet them properly. Once that ritual was performed, I explained the reason for my visit: the objects, El

Hadj Oumar's story, that of his son Ahmadou and his grandson Abdoulaye.

"I decided to come to Podor to see Fort Faidherbe. I visited it this morning and was told that you know quite a lot about the place."

He smiled.

"The fort? It's right over there," he said gesturing toward the window. I turned my head. The eyesore was indeed visible, framed by the window.

"You know? I was born right next to that fort in 1942. I grew up during the colonial period, a time when life in Podor was regulated by three sounds: the calls of the muezzin, the notes of the bugle, and the boat sirens. When you grow up in such an environment, it has an impact on you. I invested myself in the fort because I think that such a symbol needs to be conserved, for the duty of memory. France will appreciate it. Senegal will appreciate it. Africa will appreciate it, even if they do so differently, of course. We are the conquered. The French are the conquerors. Our perceptions of the fort are distinct. For us, it symbolizes French occupation and colonization. And remember, I am a former colonial subject telling you that now!"

He laughed, a mischievous giggle, and began telling me the story of the fort, as Ibrahima Sy had done that morning. And, just as I had done in the morning, I listened quietly, allowing his story to fill the room and mingle with the sounds of life carrying on around us—a neighbor's rooster, a crying baby, a pestle pounding grain in the courtyard. The story was identical, yet distinct. Each narrator added his own phrasing, his own perspective. Abdourahmane Niang's perspective focused on the fort, and his story began with this sentence, which he narrated in the form of a tale: "Podor was the meeting point between caravans and caravels, between boats and camels."

He spoke about Faidherbe, and about colonization rather than trade agreements, merchants and their houses along the quays. He explained how important Podor was to France's conquest, its strategic position along the river as a gateway to what would later become the French Sudan. He said that Faidherbe quickly understood that the French alone could not conquer Senegal, much less so Africa.

"In fact, Africa had its own weapon of mass destruction: its climate. The death toll of French troops had reached appalling proportions. So, Faidherbe asked Napoleon III to form the first regiment of Senegalese riflemen. It was created by decree on July 21, 1857. It was thanks to the Senegalese riflemen that France was able to conquer their colonial empire, which extended to the banks of the Congo River."

He went on to tell the story of the riflemen whose role was not limited to colonial conquests.

"The Maginot line. The Battle of Verdun. The Senegalese riflemen were there. At first, the Germans thought that they were French soldiers covered in grease! Then they said those savages should never come back. But they came back for the war of 1939-1945! There was this song: "The long sobs of autumn's violins wound my heart with a monotonous languor..."

Abdourahmane Niang sang Verlaine's poem, used as code by the Resistance, then sang the partisan song: "My friend, do you hear the dark flight of the crows over our plains? ..."

Outside, a mule began to bray, and the fort peered back at us through the window.

"But let's go back to Podor and the 19th century. France, which had equipped the fort and set up the regiments of riflemen, had to head east to expand its conquests. That is when their meeting with El Hadj Oumar Tall took place."

He paused for a moment, then continued as if giving a declamation: "El Hadj Oumar Tall was an extraordinary man, a scholar and holy man whose writings continue to illuminate the Arab world to this day! And in every field: poetry, literature, mysticism! To this day we have not fully examined the richness of El Hadj Oumar's works. We remember his famous trip to Mecca, on foot at the age of twenty-three. At a time when Black men were reputed for being nothing more than slaves, he braved the dangers. Back then the black man was said to belong to the lowest race, equal to toads!"

He laughed at that last bit. The kind of laughter of someone who knows better. Outside, the muezzin began to sing.

"Even in French people's memory," the old man continued, "the black man has never been considered a human being. He was a beast of burden. People even said that science was inaccessible to the black man. It's strange really, truly strange. When, whether in their anatomy or their physiology, all human beings are made up of the same elements! And yet, some believe they have the right to claim superiority over others."

He excused himself; he had to stop for prayer. He got up laboriously from his mat, sat down on a white plastic chair in front of his prayer rug and prayed in that position, his knees too painful to prostrate himself. I allowed my gaze to wander around the room at the upholstered armchairs, the desk covered with books and papers around the computer, and a small flag of Senegal on the wall, which hung above some framed awards: the Republic of Senegal's Order of Merit, the National Order of the Lion. Next to them, a painting listing El Hadj Oumar Tall's disciples with the handwritten inscription: "We have detailed our verses in honor of people gifted with knowledge, in honor of people who reason, in honor of people who reflect. The fear of God is the privilege of scholars."

After he prayed, Abdourahmane Niang turned to me. I was getting ready to leave. The time to break the fast was approaching, and it was time for me to allow him to enjoy some time with his family. But he asked me to stay.

"I'm going to finish telling my story, and then we will part ways. I want to say this: If the good Lord wanted to create a world with only French people, it would have been monotonous. But God is not uniformity. God is diversity. Human beings were created in that diversity, not to live in isolation from one another, but together. To get to know one another.

Everything that is different from me teaches and informs me. When I contrast my views with those of another, it confirms my views or else it changes them. In either case, I learn."

He separated his phrases clearly, one from the other, at times gesturing with his hands to emphasize his point.

"Any difference is enriching," he repeated. "So, relegating people to a status of nobody is unjust. Denying another's intelligence to the point of lowering him to the level of nobody is scandalous. It pushes us to extremes, like racial segregation in the United States, apartheid in South Africa, or Hitler in Europe. Planet Earth is all of ours, so we must live in harmony. We may not have the same tastes, but the other also has the right to exist. No one can live in isolation. The pandemic reminded us of that . . ."

"Colonization was that too: a hierarchy of human beings," I took the opportunity to slip in, as he paused for a moment.

"No, it is not about colonization," he disagreed. "All primitive societies felt a need to classify. Take France, for instance. You had the nobility, the clergy and the peasantry. The lord had the right to life and death in his seigneury. Our ancestors, the Gauls, as we said at school, were primitive."

His mischievous giggle resounded once again. I smiled at how he had just inverted the stigma.

"That's what I was taught: that my ancestors were Gauls," he insisted, "and that my motherland was France. Later on, we sang the Song of the Africans: 'We are the Africans who come from afar, we come from the colony to defend the country …'

But the country was always France! We sang that. Then at one point, we sang for Marshal Pétain, then De Gaulle!"

He laughed again, seeming to say that, anyway, France often changed sides.

"You see, we were molded colonial-style. Everything the white chief said was good, everything he didn't say was bad. When I was a child, at school, we had the symbol. Do you know what the symbol was? It was a wooden stick. We were forbidden to speak our mother tongue. We had to speak only French. If you were caught speaking in an African language, you were given the symbol. And you would keep it until you heard another student make the same mistake. It was an abomination to speak your own language. Can you imagine?"

As I listened to him, I could not help but think of certain teachers—in France—who still today, advised African parents not to use their mother tongue with their children, "so they could learn better French."

"I knew French geography and history like the back of my hand," Abdourahmane Niang continued. "We were not taught about Africa. El Hadj Oumar, Samory Touré . . ., all those African heroes were portrayed in such a distorted manner that we even became afraid of them. We were told that they were bloodthirsty monsters. We were terrified! Our teachers falsified history, and that is not good. A basic principle of moral probity when you teach is to teach the truth. You reproduce things as they are and leave it up to men to judge. But falsifying... The drama, for those of us who went to colonial school, is that when we learned the truth, it raised hackles."

"What does it feel like when you realize that you have been subjected to falsified history?"

"It feels bad, really bad. It was when I was at university. I remember well. That was when I became aware of it. But I said to myself: don't be resentful. There was a struggle over territory, and the French gained control. Since then, we had to move forward, put things in their rightful place, and show that we knew the real story. Africans helped to liberate France from the Germans twice. From whom did France liberate Africa? No one!"

Outside, the light was becoming increasingly oblique. The day was waning. The story was coming to an end.

"In any case, I have emptied my heart of any hate, grudges or resentment," Abdourahmane Niang concluded. "Instead, I say to myself: what if we had colonized France? What would have happened? Maybe it would have been similar. And when I hear someone like Sarkozy say in Dakar that Africans have not fully entered history, I prefer to ascribe that to ignorance. He has either forgotten or is ignoring that: ten thousand years before Jesus Christ, Egypt was the center of all sciences, and Egypt was in Africa. A Fulani proverb says: 'When you know that you do not know, you will know, but when you do not know that you do not know, you will never know.'"

THE BEGINNING OF THE STORY

HALWAR, SENEGAL, WITH THIERNO MAHMOUD TALL AND OUMAR TALL

The large room's walls were pale yellow, and its floor was covered in rugs and plastic mats with blue, orange, green and burgundy geometric patterns. Before stepping through the doorway, visitors had to remove their shoes, then sit on the floor at the back of the room, near the three mattresses covered with fabric facing the door that opened to the courtyard. In one corner of the room were piles of books and a worn-out armchair with a purple prayer rug draped over it.

A few months after I had gone to Podor, I met with Oumar Tall and his father Thierno Mahmoud Tall, heirs to El Hadj Oumar Tall's family and guardians of the religious leader's birth village, Halwar, a place of remembrance and a pilgrimage destination. It was about nine miles from National Route 2 and the crossroads town of Ndioum, which I had just left, passing by carts loaded with food, shepherds trailing their sheep, housewives with basins under their arms, all heading to the weekly Monday morning market. That day Ndioum was bustling. You had to move at a snail's pace to cross the city, avoid customers and street vendors spilling onto the road, and Jakarta motorcycles and carts that were parked waiting for passengers. Sometimes people came from far away to stock their supplies, for a bag of rice or onions, for hardware, a horse harness, or a new jacket. Some also came to sell vegetables from their garden—tomatoes, eggplants and carrots—and people took advantage of the opportunity to buy credit for their telephones and catch up on the latest news with those they knew from neighboring villages. A few years prior to my trip, to go from Ndioum to Halwar, you had to check the weather forecast before crossing two branches of the river because it becomes completely swollen during the rainy season and laterite roads make for slippery driving. Since then, the road had been newly paved, connecting the village to the national highway in less than twenty minutes and allowing the faithful to reach their destination without any trouble. During the annual pilgrimage that celebrates the birth of the religious leader, just before Ramadan, people regularly come by the busload from Dakar and the surrounding area, as well as from Mali and Guinea. El Hadj Oumar Tall's empire was vast, as was his legacy.

"Welcome," said Oumar Tall, a svelte man in his forties, dressed in white from head to toe. He sat down across from me, and his white-bearded father sat cross-legged next to him in a burgundy boubou, with an orange scarf draped over his shoulders. Thierno Mahmoud Tall was born in 1935. He was the one who told me El Hadj Oumar's story, "the part I know, namely his childhood and his pilgrimage to Mecca," to be precise, he said. He listened attentively as I explained why I had come, clicking his tongue after each sentence to indicate that he understood. Then he got up, went to find a thick green book and a notebook and sat back down cross-legged. Next to me was Ciré Harouna Ly, a young local student who had come to interpret for us. Thierno Mahmoud Tall spoke in Pulaar, as Caliph Thierno Madani had in Dakar. As the old man leafed through his notebook, we awaited the beginning of the story in reverent silence.

"Cheikh Oumar was born here, in Halwar, in around 1794," the marabout began. "He was born in the house right over there, outside. His father was polygamous. He had two wives: Adama Aïssatou and Younaïssé Abdoulaye. Adama Aïssatou was the mother of ten of his children, the youngest of whom was Cheikh Oumar. Younaïssé Abdoulaye had four of his children. Cheikh Oumar's siblings were Fatimata, Elimane Ibrahim, Oumou Kalla, Salemata, Zeinabou, Ciré, Tafsir Ansoumaye, Alpha Ahmadou, Thierno Habi as well as Aliou, Ousmane, Roukiatou and Hafsatou.

"Cheikh Oumar was born on the last day of the month before Ramadan. In Pulaar, that month is called yaawa. Remember that word: yaawa. He was born on the 29th day of that month. It was a Wednesday. So, Thursday was the first day of Ramadan. On that day, Cheikh Oumar did not suckle his mother's breast. The people had gone to see those who had wisdom to ask them questions. The wise men came to see the child to see if he was well, or if he had a problem that prevented him from suckling. They saw nothing. The baby stayed like that all day. It was only when the hour came to break the fast that he took his mother's breast. He repeated that for almost the entire month. People understood that he was fasting."

Outside, we heard the clattering of basins. The midday meal was being prepared in the courtyard. "Later, when it was time to sow the fields, Cheikh Oumar refused to sow in certain places. He said: 'I am not going to sow for the monkeys and birds. I am only going to sow what we will eat.' That came to be proven correct. Where he had sown, it had grown. Those are the mysteries of Cheikh Oumar."

A small child entered the room, carrying a piece of bread in his hand, and trotted over to us. He laid down on his back on the floor and looked over at us. Oumar Tall tickled his tummy. It was his two-year-old son, Mohamed.

"Cheikh Oumar began his studies in Halwar," Thierno Mahmoud picked up again. "First, he studied with his uncle whose name was Nguira Hamath. It was with him that he memorized the Koran. The next step included learning the rules that allow you to rewrite the Koran from memory, without looking at the book. His older brother Alpha Ahmadou was the one who taught him those. That is how Cheikh Oumar had learned the Koran. Then he left to study in Ndormboss, the village where his sister Fatima got married. He was about seven years old at the time. In Ndormboss, he learned Islamic Sharia with Lamine Sakho. After that, he went to Séno Palel. And when he returned to Halwar, he began preparations for his trip to Mecca.

"So, Cheikh Oumar came from a family of marabouts," I said.

"Yes. His father, his uncle, and his brother were marabouts."

"What distinguished him from his other brothers?"

Oumar Tall laughed and replied for his father:

"He had a God-given gift. He received wisdom from God, wisdom that is beyond books and scriptures."

"And how old was he when the others understood that he had that God-given gift?"

Thierno Mahmoud replied with an anecdote:

"Since his childhood, when Cheikh Oumar would play with the other children, it was clear that he was different in the way he spoke and what he said. He would say, for example, that he dreamed of going to Mecca and Medina. The other children didn't know what he was talking about. So, they would ask their parents: 'What is Mecca and Medina?' The parents would ask them: 'Where did you hear that?' And the children would say: 'Cheikh Oumar talks about it all the time.'

"For him, there was no doubt," Oumar Tall concluded.

"When he grew up, he would go to Mecca. He would make his pilgrimage."

"So, he stood out at a very young age," I said.

"Yes, from that moment onwards, we knew that he would be a great man. He would even ask his Koran teacher questions that the marabout did not know how to answer. He had a thirst for knowledge."

A man entered the room, knelt down next to Thierno Mahmoud, and shot me a disconcerted look.

What is a Toubab doing in this room?

The old man excused himself: "We're going to stop for a moment. This gentleman is going to travel, and he came to pray, to leave with the blessing of the marabout." Palms open toward the sky, they prayed together. Little Mohamed got up when the guest passing through arrived, approached the three men, knelt next to them, and repeated their gestures: he opened his palms toward the sky, then wiped his face with his hands. At two years old, he was familiar with the gestures that gave rhythm to his father's and grandfather's days.

"You're familiar with Podor, right?" Thierno Mahmoud continued when the guest had left. "Podor is a crossroads. That was where Cheikh Oumar met Abd el-Karim Diallo, a man who was already serving in the Tijaniyya, the brotherhood founded by Ahmed Tijani. Together, they traveled to Guinea [Conakry] and committed to make a pilgrimage to Mecca. Cheikh Oumar then headed back up to Fouta to inform his parents of his travel plan. He had arranged to meet Abd el-Karim on the Mali border so they could travel together. But, while Cheikh Oumar was in Fouta, Abd el-Karim passed away. He left Cheikh Oumar a letter telling him to continue without him. That is how he set out on his trip to Mecca alone. He passed through many countries, making several stopovers.

"Along the way, he met a certain Mohamed el-Maghrebi. He was like a king. His daughter had fallen ill. Cheikh Oumar healed her and to thank him for that miracle, Mohamed el-Maghrebi gave him a lot of gold. Cheikh Oumar continued his journey and arrived in Mecca where Mohamed el-Ghâli was his teacher. Cheikh Oumar had so much gold that for three years he was the one to provide for his teacher's daily expenses."

"At the time, were there many marabouts leaving for Mecca or was that exceptional?"

"There were some, but it was not a given for everyone. It was difficult. It was all on foot."

A few flies were buzzing around the room. The air was warm. It was almost noon. Outside, you could hear chickens clucking and a rooster crowing. The light behind the door became increasingly blinding. Oumar Tall got up and excused himself once again. He had to receive the young men who were waiting for him at the door. Their looks were as disconcerted as the former pious man who had seen me there earlier. We continued alone with his father who told me about the years that El Hadj Oumar Tall, the Tijani man who had been received by his teacher Mohamed el-Ghâli, spent in Mecca.

"After Mecca, Cheikh Oumar went to Sokoto," the old marabout continued the narrative. "That's in Nigeria. Here, in Halwar, he was believed to have died, but once he had arrived in Sokoto, he wrote a letter to his older brother Alpha Ahmadou to tell him he was alive and well. Sokoto was ruled by a certain Cheikh Ousmane Fodio, originally from a village about two miles from here. When Cheikh Oumar arrived from Mecca, Cheikh Ousmane Fodio had already died, and his son Mohamed Bello ruled the kingdom. He was the one who taught Cheikh Oumar warfare."

"So, those were important years?"

"Yes. He fought for seven years with Mohamed Bello who was waging a holy war. That is where he learned everything he needed to know about war."

"And that was also where he got married?"

"Yes. Cheikh Ousmane Fodio had said that once Cheikh Oumar came back, he would have to be given a wife. Blessed would be all those who were united with him!"

"And what happened after Sokoto?"

"He came back here, to Halwar, in 1840. Then, in 1845, he left for Guinea, with 87 disciples. It was in Guinea, in Dinguiraye, that he formed his army and launched his holy war to fight the enemies of Islam."

"The enemies of Islam, were they mostly the Bambara kingdoms?"

"There were many enemies. Here, in Fouta, there were no enemies, but there were things that had to be made clear.

People here practiced Islam, but they were also practicing other things that had to be fought. And there were enemies who did not believe in Islam, from Guinea to Mali."

"What were the practices that were unclear?"

The old man laughed.

"For instance, the Fulani who tattooed their lips. That is not part of Islam. It is difficult to respect all the rules of Islam. Even now, we see behaviors that do not respect Islam. People tend to adopt Western behaviors and leave religion aside. Like the women who wear skirts that are too short."

"What happened with the Bambara kingdoms that were not Muslim?"

"Cheikh Oumar extolled armed force. If you refused Islam, he would fight you. That's what happened."

"And what about fetishes, objects that were related to practices that contradicted Islam? What did Cheikh Oumar do with those?"

"I was not born there, and I have never set foot there, so I do not know. But what I do know is that he fought against those practices. When he found people who did not pray, who consumed alcohol, he fought them. That is how he conquered Ségou and other kingdoms. And after Ségou, he fought Macina, where one part of the population did not pray. He waged war on them to integrate them into Islam. But my knowledge of all that is limited."

Oumar Tall returned. He sat on the mat and directed his words at me.

"Is it Ségou that interests you most?"

"Yes, that's right. In particular what happened to the objects that were taken from there and what happened to Ahmadou's son Abdoulaye."

"What I know of the story is this: a person spoke to Archinard's troops and revealed a secret that allowed the troops to enter Ségou. They arrived at Ahmadou's palace, but found only women and Ahmadou's young son, Abdoulaye, who fought back. That was when Archinard said to himself: this boy is a great warrior. He must not be killed. He must be captured. And that is what they did. They took the saber too, the one that was in Abdoulaye's hands. But this is important: it was not really El Hadj Oumar Tall's saber, as the French say it is! It was one of Ahmadou's sabers."

"Some also say that El Hadj Oumar Tall did not even have a saber..."

"No, that is not true. He had a saber, but that saber was in Bandiagara. He actually had several sabers, because no one wages war with only one weapon."

He paused for a moment, then resumed:

"Some of the stories that interest you are unpleasant to hear, because what trumped everything was the law of the strongest. That is what happened between the white people and the black people. The whites were stronger, better armed. Cheikh Oumar never wanted to fight the white people. He wanted to build a Muslim empire that was distinctly Islamic, with no obstacles. That is why he left

Dinguiraye and headed east. Then the whites attacked him. They wanted to destroy his army. That is how that went. It is a long story."

A silence settled between us. Outside the birds began to chirp.

"And what about Abdoulaye? Did the French write something about him?" Oumar Tall asked.

"Not to my knowledge. A lot of French people think that colonial history has nothing to do with them, because they were not there themselves. However, many French cities were built from the wealth of the colonial empire: Bordeaux, Nantes, and Marseille, for example. Nowadays, the French don't even know who Faidherbe or Archinard were."

"Really? But they are French!"

"That is true. But that history is not taught in French schools. I think people in Senegal are more familiar with Faidherbe and Archinard than in France."

"Really? What we want to do here is establish a documentation center with the archives. So, when someone wants to do research on Cheikh Oumar, they can come and consult the archives. We do not have a lot of resources, and it is complicated, because people are of different minds. The governments are different. There is Senegal, Mali, and Guinea. But it is time that we too benefit from this legacy, that his descendants get their eyes on it."

I thought about my history lessons in primary school, which I learned in a Senegalese school.

"And what about El Hadj Oumar Tall's death? How is it told here? Because I remember my lessons…"

"He died mysteriously in the cliffs of Bandiagara," the young student next to me recited from memory, smiling. "That story is told so well! When they tell us that story in fifth grade, you feel like you yourself are at war."

His smile was that of an amazed child listening to stories about heroes. "That is how we tell it, too," Oumar Tall continued. When Cheikh Oumar wanted to leave, he bequeathed all his wisdom to one person. Then he said: 'I'm leaving.' And no one has seen him since. No one can say: he left this way, or he went that way. That is the story as we know it."

The interview was coming to an end. Little Mohamed had gone out, come back, gone out again, scampering around between the living room and the courtyard, the adults watching him out of the corner of their eyes.

"Will you stay for lunch? And for tea afterwards?"

It was unacceptable to say no to hospitality here. As we waited for the food, I asked if it would be possible to see El Hadj Oumar Tall's house and the mosque.

"Do you practice Islam?"

"No, I am not Muslim."

"Then you can look in through the door."

Outside, it was starting to get very hot. We walked across the courtyard of the family compound and passed through the main gate to where the guide was born. It was a simple mud house. One of the three wooden doors was open. A curtain flapped gently in the breeze wafting into the room. Inside, the ground was completely covered with a plastic mat on top of which was a large Oriental rug. Rustic wooden beams supported the ceiling, and a tiny skylight let in a sliver of light in the back of the room.

"This is where he was born. During the pilgrimage, everyone wants to come in. Cheikh Oumar learned to write Arabic under that tree over there in front of the house."

Next to the tree, a newer building made of concrete blocks stood out. It was a conference center that was established in 2014 to welcome the faithful. The contrast with the mud hut was striking. On the other side of the compound, in front of the small mosque with yellow walls, built in the same traditional style as the house, an awning had been added. Its roof was made of sheet metal and there was a cement floor beneath it.

"It was not well-made," Oumar Tall said shaking his head. "It doesn't look like the mosque, and besides, it is falling into disrepair. In the rainy season, it fills with water."

The asphalt road stopped directly in front of the mosque's awning, a rectilinear black outline against the ocher landscape, surrounded by thatched roofed huts. Behind the mosque, satellite dishes protruded from the roof, pointing toward the nearest transmitter.

TWO LITTLE SNAKES

DAKAR, SENEGAL
NATIONAL ARCHIVES

The yellowed sheet of paper was crumpled along its edges. A few tiny bits of it came loose and slid onto the brown linoleum table when I opened file #1D101 from Senegal's National Archives, titled "Sudan Campaign, 1889-1890." When I entered the reading room, I left the hustle and bustle of Dakar behind me and went back in time to Archinard's era. On the paper was a hand-drawn map of Ségou, "according to Mage and Marchand, scale 1:5,000," the legend read. Blue for the Niger River, a red dotted line for the fortress built along the water, pink that looked like a trace of watercolor for the Somonos village—Bambara fishermen—and the villages of the captives on either side of the citadel.

A young naval officer, Eugène Mage had been sent to Ségou at the end of 1863, mandated by Governor Faidherbe, to negotiate a treaty with El Hadj Oumar Tall authorizing the French to build forts along the Niger River. The only person

Mage found there, though, was Ahmadou, El Hadj Oumar Tall's son. The religious leader had left to fight troops from Timbuktu near Bandiagara, where he had succumbed a few months later. The negotiations with Ahmadou proved to be long and tedious—so long and tedious that Mage was stuck on site for twenty-six months. In the end, Ahmadou refused France's proposal, simply offering them to protect their trade in exchange for a 10% tax on goods in transit through his empire. So, from Faidherbe's point of view, those were twenty-six months spent for very little in return. But for young Mage, who was thought to have died in Saint-Louis, with no news from him for so long, twenty-six months gave him plenty of time to observe the local habits and customs, make sketches, and take notes, all of which would later be used to draw this map for the needs of the military campaign that Archinard would lead twenty-six years later. Red lines drawn inside the fortress demarcated the "Al Hagui's diounfoutou" [palace], "Ahmadou's diounfoutou" and, nearby, the gunpowder depot. In Al Hagui's diounfoutou, a small red square caught my eye. "Treasure," said the text written next to it. In his book, *A Journey to French Sudan*, Mage estimated the value of the treasure to be worth 20 million francs. He described it as the loot El Hadj Oumar Tall got his hands on by seizing the Bambara kingdom of Ségou in 1861.

The treasure would then be mentioned in all of France's other missions to Ségou: Paul Soleillet's in 1878 and Joseph Gallieni's at the end of 1880, both of whom had left to negotiate exclusive trade between the Toucouleur and the French, to the detriment of the English. Neither would succeed. Relations with Ahmadou, who had led the empire since the death of his father, were increasingly tense, to the extent that Gallieni would not even manage to be received in Ségou. Accused by Ahmadou of having gone to see his enemies of the Bambara kingdoms on his way, he would have to be stationed forty kilometers away from the city.

In their mission report, Soleillet, just like Gallieni, reported the treasure—which they, nor Eugène Mage had never even seen—thus cultivating a myth that was found in the oral tradition of the region. The control over the "Treasure of Ségou" seemed to be a symbol of power at once for the French and the Toucouleur Empires. Gallieni estimated its value first at "a few million," affirming then, before members of the Commercial Geography Society of Bordeaux—where "the intrepid explorer" had been invited for "an intimate conversation" about his mission to Ségou—that [its value] could be as high as "one hundred million."

One of the office members also pointed out to Gallieni that he had "probably set foot on the richest land in the world." He thought of the gold in Bouré and in Bambouk, mines which were close to Ségou. They fueled all the fantasies in the region and perhaps even more so in France.

Like all rumors, the one about the Treasure of Ségou swelled. Archinard was certainly aware of it when he prepared his troops to take the city. I looked at the more than one hundred-thirty-year-old crumpled sheet of paper sitting on the table in the reading room in Dakar and imagined the captain hovering over it. He had taken command of the troops in 1888 and was convinced that the peaceful colonial policy Paris had wanted was destined to fail. So Archinard thought that Ahmadou had to be taken out, just as the King of the Wassoulou Empire, Samory Touré, had to be taken out, also for threatening France's power. Aware that he was in complete disagreement with a government that did not want an expensive war, Archinard made his decisions alone, presenting his superiors a fait accompli. That was how in February, 1889 he ordered the destruction of the fort in Koundian, which belonged to Ahmadou. He only informed the governor in Saint-Louis after the fact, maintaining that the act was inevitable. He constantly forced Paris's hand, was convinced that his strategy was the best and that negotiations would lead to nothing.

In his military report, which I dove into a few days later, Archinard retraced the course of his past operations and justified his decisions. He explained that Ahmadou was working on an alliance with other kingdoms who opposed the French, an alliance which was about to prevail and had to be suppressed at all costs. Anticipating criticism, he wrote:

It was time for us to organize our new colony, make it productive, collect taxes and earn revenue. It had to come to the aid of the metropolis which had been making heavy sacrifices for it for ten years. Besides, any organization would be impossible given the neighboring vicinity and Ahmadou's hostility.

Essentially: if France lost money in her colonies, it was Ahmadou's fault, not Archinard's. What a way to manipulate the narrative, I thought to myself, my nose buried in the report. Especially in his position as senior commander of troops, it was probably quite something to think that a treasure awaited him in Ségou, a treasure that was worth millions if not a hundred million francs.

When I looked up, I saw that the reading room had filled up. The security guard at the entrance had dozed off behind his desk as he waited for his lunch hour or the next request form for a document. He was the one who received the requests, then he would bring them to the archivists who, in turn, dove into the maze of reserves on the other side of the glass partition separating them from the reading room. Next to the security guard were metal storage cabinets, whose small drawers were filled with card stock cards, one for each reference. Research was carried out using those file cards, not a database or digital catalogue. I took pleasure in physically touching the paper and leafing through inventories, opening files and registers, and examining each page. It was a guilty pleasure, especially when the cover indicated: "Fragile Document: handle with extreme care." I thought to myself: each hand that touches them, including my own, damaged them a little bit more.

For several days, I traveled back through a few years of Archinard's life like that, through military documents, march logs and operation reports, and his correspondence registries with the governor or the minister. I detected no trace of the familiar tone of the letters I had read in Saint-Louis, letters that Archinard had sent to his brother in France, which were reproduced in the book written in his honor. Here, there was neither mention of undergarments nor the dinner menu. Those everyday anecdotes had nothing to do with the telegrams sent to the governor or the reports written about the progress of the ground operations. I struggled to decipher the handwriting that dated back more than one hundred years. At times I got bored going through pages and pages detailing the military's daily life, for instance a day's march, reported hour by hour, such as one that occurred on March 27, 1890, as the troops were advancing toward Ségou:

>Depart 0335, march until 0445.
>Halt from 0445 to 0500.
>March from 0500 to 0600.
>Halt from 0600 to 0615.
>March from 0615 to 0705.
>Halt from 0705 to 0720.
>March from 0720 to 0810.
>Halt from 0810 to 0820.
>March from 0820 to 0855.

At 9 o'clock AM at the latest, the military column would stop. It was much too hot by then. I read weeks and weeks of detailed reports, some of which included personal remarks about the landscape: "beautiful trees," "lovely sacred grove." The author seemed to appreciate nature and one hundred-thirty years later, I was thanking him for those little details that brightened up my reading because—let's admit it—it was often soporific. I resisted the temptation to skip pages. I thought to myself: I would not have been a very good historian.

Suddenly, one letter jumped out at me as I was reading a correspondence register between Archinard and the governor. Dated October 28, 1889, in Kayes, five months before Ségou was captured, it was about the fate of Mamadou Lamine's two sons. Lamine was a marabout who had sown unrest in the country a few years earlier, planning to establish his own state and liberate the region from both the French and the Toucouleur. Ahmadou and Gallieni had become occasional allies in the fight against their common enemy, whom the French troops had killed in December 1887. His two sons had been taken prisoner and sent to the School for Hostages in Kayes, according to customary practices of that time. The eldest was then sixteen years old, and Archinard was worried about his future—but in somewhat particular terms.

> *It is vexing for the tranquility of the country that these children were not killed in battle or that we did not completely expatriate them, but now there is hardly*

any way to go back on our benevolent measure. We have raised two little snakes. They are intelligent, speak French fairly correctly, and can write it in an understandable way. And in spite of the concern that we have shown for them, they see themselves as prisoners and aspire only to the time when they will take their final leave from our school to go to perfect their study of the Koran and the sacred books and become great marabouts and leaders of holy wars, just like their father.

They are the object of veneration of nearly everyone, and now that the eldest is sixteen or seventeen, the villages have begun to send him women to marry. I did not authorize the marriages since the parents had acknowledged that the boy was still much too young and that his family would save those fiancés for him.

The village chiefs and their relatives have been taking steps for some time to have the eldest child, whom they wanted to turn into a marabout, left to them [...] I had the children brought to my office before those who asked for them, I had them write a few lines of dictation, and I altered their leave date to a few months later, with the pretext that they were not yet educated sufficiently in French. I added that I saw no problem in them becoming marabouts and that we ourselves had sent marabouts, like Bou el-Moghdad, to Mecca.

Regarding my personal situation, I am absolutely convinced that those children whom I've known for a year, as well as the company they keep and the feelings people manifest toward them, will before long be adversaries for us, and they pose a particular danger since they have lived among us. I only see one way to rid ourselves of those two preachers of holy war who will undoubtedly pose new problems to some of my successors and will impose new insurrections we will need to quell, and that is to send those two young men to a high school in Paris. There, they will become French enough to no longer worry about holy war and could become valuable civil servants. In any case, living among us for a few years would take any religious prestige away from them in the eyes of their compatriots.

I have the honor to request, Mr. Governor, that you kindly forward this letter to Mr. Deputy Secretary of State of the Colonies. It is my great desire that it be taken into consideration. If it is not, I am convinced that the future will demonstrate quite quickly that I am not mistaken. However, my interest in this matter is not personal, and if Mr. Deputy Secretary of State does not share my view, I will return the children to their family, who are begging for their return. I would simply ask that a rapid reply come to dictate my behavior.

I have the honor, Mr. Governor, to be your respectful and obedient servant.

The violence of the words he used to describe the two boys astounded me, but perhaps even more disturbing was how violent his plan was, how carefully thought through and meticulously detailed it was: to cut off the children not only from their family, but also from their culture, their language and their country, to destroy every last trace of the history that informed their identity. I thought of what Ndiabou Séga Touré had said at El Hadj Oumar Foutiyou Tall High School: "If you do not know where you come from, it is difficult for you to know where you are headed." For Archinard, the best way to protect the interests of France in the colony was to make it so those children no longer knew where they came from. The School for Hostages was no longer enough. They had to take the next step: exile in France. That was Abdoulaye's fate when he was captured in Ségou five months later.

A few letters later, on January 8, 1890, Archinard wrote again to the governor about Mamadou Lamine's two sons. He had another request to forward to the undersecretary, "a fact of little significance to us, but which could have some importance for those children": what to do with their father's head. In fact, it is said that his head had been shown to his children so they would "walk straight." The author of that "joke"—in Archinard's words—was Captain Fortin who had claimed that, besides, he himself had beheaded him. "Quite a gross error, especially since it was not Captain Fortin who cut off his head, but Moussa Molo's and Sountoukouma's people," Archinard pointed out, noting that that was enough to spark the hatred those boys harbored toward France.

But the problem, Archinard added, remained elsewhere. The problem was the children's planned departure for France. Furthermore, "Lieutenant-Colonel Gallieni was careful to have their father's head precede them."

I do not know what happened to that head, which all the newspapers had written about, Archinard went on. It was most certainly given to the Museum as an anthropological object and must be on display in some case with a label.

The commander worried about what that might have triggered on a playground. He wrote:

As a school prank, the marabout's children's classmates could well renew the stupidity committed by Captain Fortin or a similar stupidity, and it might be good if Mr. Under-Secretary of State, if he would, ask the Museum administration to please not exhibit that head for the public or, if they were really interested in doing so, to at least please not put a label on it.

Later, I searched the online inventory of the Natural History Museum's collections of biological anthropology in Paris. In the "Modern Human Remains" section, the keywords

"Mamadou" and "Lamine" gave zero search results. But when I typed Senegal, I came across a list of one hundred-fourteen references, all indexing skulls. Nothing indicated to me whether that of Mahdi and Abdoul Bassar's father was still there.

ARCHINARD'S HOSTAGES

DAKAR, SENEGAL
NATIONAL ARCHIVES

The blackmail began three days after the city was sieged. On April 9, 1890, from Ségou, Archinard wrote to Ahmadou:

> *You did not want to recognize our borders. You did not want to allow trade [to take place] on the Niger. Your son wrote to me that he was mocking us as if we were a mosquito buzzing in his ears. I will punish you for that by taking away your capital and returning it to those from whom your father had taken it. Then, depending on your behavior, I will see what else I will do.*

The letter was drafted on French Republic letterhead. The paper had become yellowed and speckled over time. On the table in front of me was a pile of those letters, written in French then translated into Arabic, the language in which

Ahmadou and Archinard communicated. There were also Ahmadou's replies, A5-sized sheets of paper filled with beautiful calligraphy. The pages were folded into small squares with the markings of the folds still visible on the paper.

I spent some long days in the reading room of the National Archives of Senegal going through registers, maps and correspondences and immersing myself in military documents that corresponded chronologically. That was how I began to retrace the course of events between April and July of 1890. I found out that the day Archinard sent that letter to Ahmadou, on April 9th, he also gave orders to all post commanders to shoot their cannons eleven times for the siege of Ségou. It was order #422, recorded in a register with a cardboard cover which grouped together Archinard's orders between October 13, 1889, and July 24, 1890. I also learned that the city fell on April 6th, its fall recounted minute by minute in the march journal and operations log. It was Easter Sunday, the author noted in the margins, next to the date.

On that day, the military column had arrived on the banks of the Niger River at 5:25 AM. Opposite, on the other side of the water, no one seemed too concerned about the troops' presence, which included Senegalese riflemen and French soldiers.

Women are going to the water. Warriors are coming out little by little in arms. The Somonos (Bambara fishermen) rapidly raising their nets are returning to the right bank. Although Ségou Sikasso knows that the Nyamina military column is departing, he looks surprised. The inhabitants and their leader, Madani, do not seem to believe that we can attack them.

I read the author's descriptions. He was a keen observer (was it the same person who had noted the lovely sacred grove and the beautiful trees?). I imagined the scene, remembering the map drawn according to Mage's indications, the loop that made this place the Niger River, with the Somonos village across on the left and Ahmadou's diounfoutou on the right. The king was not in Ségou. He was cornered in Nioro, two hundred fifty miles away as the crow flies, cut off from his town by pockets of Bambara resistance who were blocking his way. He had settled there to manage some of the kingdom's internal conflicts which had lasted for several years already. So, his son Madani was governing in Ségou. "[His] house on the riverbank is easily decipherable, for it stands out with its white color and upper level," the author noted.

The battle was being prepared with neither noise nor fanfare, except for the sound of the tabala, the drum that announced danger, which alerted the inhabitants of Ségou at 6:30 AM. Armed riders on horseback were leaving the city as the colonial troops proceeded to encounter the ford. "Impossible to cross on foot," Captain Mamadou Racine decreed. "We need dugout canoes." At 9:15 AM, France's cannons launched their first shots on the city, frightening the inhabitants. No shots fired back at them; guns did not carry that far. At 11:45 AM, the son of the Somonos leader crossed the river to announce the submission of his village to the French. Barely one hour later, several other Somonos arrived to warn the French that the Toucouleur were fleeing. Immediately afterward, at 12:35 PM, the order was given "to cross the river and go occupy the treasure." I paused at the handwritten word, to make sure I had deciphered it correctly. Yes, I had. It indeed said "occupy the treasure"—not the city. Archinard knew exactly what he had come for.

At 1:45 PM Ségou was under occupation, "except for Ahmadou's tata (fort) whose doors were closed." After he had hoisted a man up into a tree to observe what was going on behind the surrounding wall, Archinard gave the order to break down the doors with two cannon shots. Inside, there were only women and children: Ahmadou's wives, his sister, his two sons as well as Madani's wife and only son. Among the group was young Abdoulaye, who Archinard describes in detail in his military report, which he wrote later:

> *Only one of Ahmadou's young sons, Abdoulaye, a beautiful child about twelve years old, refused to leave and separate from his mother. He came back to the city, reentered the diounfoutou where one of his youngest brothers was already. Today, he is in our hands. Away from all those arrogant and cruel Toucouleur who act so harshly, with all their treachery and domination over*

the braver yet more naïve populations, one child alone and a few women showed courage.

Was it at that moment, in that very first confrontation with the child, that Archinard decided that he would have to be sent to France? He made no mention of it in his report, and the march newspaper as well as the correspondence registers say nothing about it either. Indeed, there was something much more urgent: find the treasure.

The search began April 6th, as soon as the tata's doors had been forced open. The search began near El Hadj's house, where Mage had located the treasure, but it resulted in nothing. Three days later, on April 9th, while Archinard was writing his first letter to Ahmadou and giving the order to fire the cannon to celebrate the siege of the city, the author of the march journal noted: "The search for the treasure is in vain."

It was only on the following day, on April 10th, that the troops managed to get their hands on the loot: "At four o'clock," wrote the same author, "the treasure's guard, Bakary, whom the police commissioner had found in Nyamina, indicated that the treasure had been buried in a miserable-looking hut which served as the country's dabas (tool) store."

The search thus resumed at the indicated location, six feet deep, at night. Before long, with the six soldiers who were present, including Captains Bonnier, Quinquandon and Racine, they had hoisted out of the ground six bundles made of ox hide and canvas, inside of which was jewelry—the same jewelry that would later be exhibited in Paris and had survived two thefts, first at the Army Museum, then at the Palais de la Porte Dorée—and which is stored to this day at the Quai Branly Museum. The hides and the canvas had rotted, the author explained, and the gold and silver were mixed with soil. He noted: "Without being able to specify, we can estimate the whole at a value ranging between two hundred and two hundred-fifty thousand francs."

Suffice it to say, it was far from the one hundred million estimated by Gallieni, and even from Mage's twenty million. In his military report, Archinard appeared to be very disappointed. And as was often the case, in his style that I was beginning to identify by dint of going through documents, he placed the blame on others to justify himself, and those others were most often Africans. They were the ones who had provided false information to Mage in his time, the troop commander implied: "It is indeed the case here to apply the coefficient reduction admitted by Lieutenant-Colonel Desbordes, who divided the figures the blacks had given by ten to get closer to the truth."

On April 11th, the day after the treasure was found then quickly stored in nailed shut ammunition boxes and placed under surveillance, Ahmadou's wives and sons were transported by dugout canoe to the other riverbank. On the 17th, they left for Kita, far from the combat zones, in a convoy led by Captain Mamadou Racine. The crates of jewels as well as the manuscripts, also seized on site, were loaded into Lefebvre cars and sent to Bafoulabé, pulled by mules. The loot was then loaded into the train headed toward Kayes—the railway had made good progress since Archinard's arrival ten years earlier.

And the blackmail continued. Archinard had a message sent to Ahmadou explaining the conditions for finding his family: he had to renounce his power and go into exile in a village near Dinguiraye, in what is today Guinea, "and again, it will be forbidden for [him] to slit anyone's throat—not even a captive or a woman—without asking permission from his superior." Otherwise, the war would continue, "until [he] is either killed or out of the way."

"The word of a French leader is sacred," the troop commander added.

Ahmadou replied that all he had to do was free the women first, and he would discuss afterward.

"Actions speak louder than words."

Were those the words of a French leader, I wanted to add as I deciphered the translation.

Obviously, none of the women were freed. Quite the opposite. Archinard's troops were already marching on Ouéssébougou, also held by the Toucouleur. The city was taken on April 26th, after murderous fighting, unlike in Ségou where the colonial troops had recorded no deaths or injuries. In that second battle, the description of which goes on for nineteen pages of the march journal, there were fifteen dead and sixty-eight injured on the French side, which was detailed in the journal according to their origins: white people were mentioned by their names; black people were merely numbers. The latter were seven times more numerous among the injured. Thus, in the city, on the enemy's side, French troops recorded three hundred dead. They also found the tabala, the drum they had heard several times during the fighting. Reclaimed by Archinard, that object would end up in the permanent collection of the Natural History Museum of Le Havre, placed in a display case by the commander himself thirty-nine years later, in 1929, with the title "Ahmadou's drum." The skin of the instrument had been deliberately slit so it could never make a sound again. Slashed as a symbol of a bloody victory, I would later think to myself, when I saw the drum. If I had not known its history, would I have even paid attention to it?

On May 15th, when the convoy of women had just arrived in Kita after a month-long march, Archinard made another attempt with Ahmadou. The letter repeated the conditions set forth as such: go into exile in a village near Dinguiraye and renounce all power. In exchange, his life would be spared, and he would see some of his family again.

Did Archinard seriously think he would have the slightest chance of getting that from Ahmadou? I could not believe it. The tone of his letters made me think more of someone who was taunting his opponent whom he wanted to humiliate. Besides, the tone hardened two weeks later; they had become open threats.

I sought to agree with you by keeping the peace and

setting your borders. You did not want that. You incited all the leaders of the countries to act against us. I waged war on you. God has abandoned you. Now that everyone can see that we are the strongest, I believed I could show that we are good and that we only wage war when we are forced to do so. I sent you three emissaries through Moumar Diak, and I sent another one through Abdoul Cadi, to speak sincerely with you because I never lie. I offered you your life, a village and your family. You responded with only a letter to Moumar Diak. I recognize neither your seal nor Seydou Delia's handwriting. They are meaningless to me.

Now, all those people I have brought back from Ségou are costing me too much to feed and maintain. I have been far too generous. I warn you one last time. If I do not have an answer from you in the time it takes to receive my correspondence, I will dispose of the people in your family whom I have treated with respect and have placed in no one's hands. I will scatter them so far and wide that you no longer have any hope of seeing them again. I will send some to Gabon. I will give others to the Bambara who live in the middle of Bélédougou so that you cannot reach them. I will send your two sons to France just like I sent Mamadou Lamine's two sons four months ago. I do not know how many of them they are; there are many, but here are the names of some of them.

A detailed list followed: Ahmadou's wives, his mother, his sister, his daughter, and his sons. And in lieu of a signature, one last threat: "I will await your reply, but I will not wait long. Good-bye."

So Mamadou Lamine's two children had endured forced exile in France. What happened to them afterward? Was there some trace of them somewhere, on a yellowed piece of paper I had not consulted, on a digitized document in some database, in a hardbound register kept on reserve, somewhere between West Africa and France?

Since I had progressed with my research, I had come across the names of riflemen, interpreters, women and children of defeated leaders, names of white soldiers, of traders, nurses, gardeners, cooks... I scrolled through all those names, which sometimes came back as I leafed through a conduct report, a military report, or a letter to a brother in France, and I thought about all those lives they represented. Each name was a thread that connected France to West Africa. I saw them woven together for four centuries, like a piece of fabric connecting the memory and the body of each individual, things that were either transmitted or kept silent, that were exhumed or buried. A memory, a secret, a name. A photo, an object, a bit of DNA.

After five o'clock, when the archives closed, I went back out into the din of Avenue Malick Sy, amidst the honking taxis, the putt-putting, backfiring Jakarta motorcycles, and the screeching tires of the Tata buses. Before cutting through the chaotic traffic and returning to where I was staying in the Ilot Alter neighborhood next to the old wooden houses, I felt as though I was part of that crowd of individuals coming to life through my research. Each day, there were more of them. Each day the plot developed, though I did not know what exact direction it was taking, whether their destinies had merely crossed, intertwined, or been forced, and if the fabric of their lives had been woven to expose its front or its underside. Every encounter created two possible versions of history, that of the conqueror and that of the conquered, that of the guest and that of the host, that of the author of the narrative and that of the protagonist. I fell asleep to their voices, which would sometimes crop up in my dreams.

As I was getting up in the morning, I heard the birds and the washerwomen next door getting to work, scrubbing the laundry and the sound of the water splashing into their basins. I heard the muezzin of Dakar's Great Mosque nearby and, behind it in the bustling background of a city that never sleeps, the muffled sounds of National Highway 1 a few hundred yards away. I went out into the street, grabbed a Touba coffee and dove back into the archives.

The convoy transporting the Treasure of Ségou arrived in Kayes at the end of May 1890. A commission made up of an artillery captain, an assistant commissioner and a pharmacist was designated to open the crates, carry out a preliminary sorting and weigh the gold under the treasurer of Kayes's supervision. According to the official classification report, which I would consult later in other archives in Aix-en-Provence, out of one hundred sixty pounds of gold, only thirteen pounds of jewelry would be considered of sufficient interest to be sent to France. It was the same for the silver artifacts: of the three hundred forty-six pounds they found, only one crate containing thirteen pounds of them would leave for Paris. The rest were sold at auction in Kayes three weeks later. After the sale, Archinard gave the order to package everything that was to be sent to France. Regarding the five hundred eighteen manuscripts recovered in Ségou, he specified: "The separate book pages will be stacked and packaged without sorting. The books will be sorted and classified into three categories: the Koran, religious books, and history."

A few days earlier, Ahmadou's family had reached Kayes by train. While en route, the convoy suffered two attacks from Toucouleur horsemen whom Archinard described in his military report. I deciphered his handwriting as I thought of young Abdoulaye on board: the loaded train slowing down on an uphill slope, the boy hearing the troops loyal to his father galloping behind the railway car, getting closer and closer, in hopes of being freed, the riflemen getting down to fire, the locomotive picking up speed, and Abdoulaye who resigned himself to failure, once, then a second time.

June 21st, the day the women and children arrived in Kayes, was also the day the tabala—which had sounded the alert in Ouéssébougou—was placed on display in the city. That did not seem to be by chance. Human beings, just like the torn leather drum, were spoils of war.

One month later, on July 23rd, Archinard sent a telegram to the governor of Senegal detailing how he intended to distribute Ahmadou's wives to other leaders for them to marry. He described each woman in a few words—"a wonderful girl," "a nice girl," "another very beautiful young woman, almost white," "very attractive." Some were accompanied by their mothers or children. Twenty-seven people were dispersed like that. Regarding Abdoulaye, Archinard had another plan, which he revealed in that cable:

> *I will bring Ahmadou's son to Saint-Louis. He is about twelve years old, a very handsome young man, almost European. It is nearly impossible for me to give him away or leave him here. He has been under my care for a long time. I propose entrusting him to an officer on my general staff during his stay in Saint-Louis, then sending him to France.*

The fate of the loot was thus sealed. Archinard added: "I also have eight little girls for the head of the justice department and four for the Protestant mission. If you find you need more of one group, I could increase those numbers a little."

Who were those little girls? Captives from Ségou? Children whom chiefs had given as a gift as a means of signing a treaty or an accord? In all the documents I have gone through, there were dozens and dozens of women and children who had changed hands in that way, been sent here and there, offered or captured, women and children whose destiny no longer belonged to them. It almost made me think that Abdoulaye, who spent time with Archinard, was perhaps lucky.

As I closed the last document of 1890, I was baffled. I had combed through Archinard's telegram and correspondence registers, the march logs and the military reports, and I had not seen any mention of one object which had otherwise made a great deal of noise during the past weeks and whose story was linked to Ségou.

That object was the saber attributed to El Hadj Oumar Tall, conserved in the collections of the Army Museum in Paris, which the French Prime Minister Édouard Philippe had just "returned" to Senegal. Quotation marks are necessary here since, according to French law, any artwork from a public collection can neither be given nor returned unless it is taken out of the collection by a specific law—which was not the case of the saber. So, officially, it was a five-year loan, but Édouard Philippe's speech in Dakar in mid-November of 2019 indeed mentioned a "restitution procedure." There was nothing trivial about the timing. The saber was already in Dakar, on loan for a year for the inaugural exhibition at the Museum of Black Civilizations, a brand-new museum financed by Chinese funding, which opened its doors in the Senegalese capital in December, 2018. When Édouard Philippe proceeded with the "restitution," the loan agreement was about to end, and the saber had to go back to the Army Museum.

In France, however, Emmanuel Macron's declarations about returning African heritage sparked a virulent debate which continued for two years between those demanding unconditional restitution and those who feared seeing museums empty out. A report commissioned by the president, written by French art historian Bénédicte Savoy and Senegalese economist Felwine Sarr, added fuel to the fire: the authors unequivocally recommended that the stolen art be returned. As an example, they cited the loot from Ségou, including the saber from the Army Museum, the jewelry from the Quai Branly and the objects from the Natural History Museum of Le Havre.

It was therefore probably not a coincidence that the first piece to be "returned" by France was precisely that weapon, already exhibited twice in Dakar before the loan in 2018. The first time was in 1998, during the bicentenary of El Hadj Oumar Tall's birth, and the second was in 2008, for an exhibition at the Théodore Monod African Art Museum in Dakar. It was an object that the Senegalese public knew and eagerly awaited. They knew that heroic tale of the saber that Archinard had ripped out of young Abdoulaye's hands as the latter defended his mother, brandishing it before the colonial troops who had entered Ahmadou's tata. But the question was: if that saber was part of the loot from Ségou and really belonged to El Hadj Oumar Tall, why was there absolutely no mention of this otherwise highly symbolic object in any of the documents I had just gone through for weeks? Perhaps I had missed something. Otherwise, where was the saber?

THE GEOPOLITICS OF MEANING

DAKAR, SENEGAL
THE MUSEUM OF BLACK CIVILIZATIONS

The small statuette stared back at me through wide, marble-like eyes. Her upper body was covered with geometric scarifications, with breasts pointed like cones and a protruding navel. A necklace made of tiny glass beads adorned her waist, wrists and left ankle. Standing barely a foot and a half tall, the structure had been placed in the first row of the display case, leaving in front of the three other human statuettes behind it, as if she was meant to take center stage. Her name, Nyeleni, meant "little favorite."

I had entered the Museum of Black Civilizations in Dakar to see El Hadj Oumar Tall's saber, but the first object that caught my attention was the "little favorite" and her wide eyes. "Gift from General Archinard, 1929," the plate indicated.

In the room dedicated to "African civilizations" I noticed several other pieces that Archinard had donated. An ebony mask with refined features, its slender face extending upward into several spikes, like a headdress. A crest in the shape of an antelope, a shape I've been familiar with since childhood because I have seen it reproduced so many times in logos or on souvenir objects offered to tourists. Musical instruments: a five-hole flute, a n'goni guitar, a soku fiddle. All of them had been donated to the Natural History Museum of Le Havre in 1929, three years before Archinard's death. They had made the trip to Dakar for a one-year loan.

I looked at those Bambara cultural objects, which were connected to the animist practices that El Hadj Oumar Tall fought against in his jihad, destroying the fetishes and other objects of divination deemed incompatible with Islam. Unlike the objects taken in Ségou and sent directly to the museums in Paris as early as 1890, those objects had first been part of Archinard's personal collections, and they had remained at the general's residence for thirty or forty years, in his Paris apartment in the 17th arrondissement or else in the private mansion he had acquired on Boulevard de Strasbourg, a few steps from the Le Havre train station.

With the "little favorite" staring back at me with her wide eyes, I thought about the thousands of miles she had traveled to reach the places she had lived over the past one hundred thirty years, from the time she had left the territory that is present-day Mali, traveling all the way to Paris, then arriving in Le Havre, moving from the general's home to a museum before being placed on reserve, then wrapped up in a crate headed to Dakar and placed in the display case that stood now before me, for a one-year stay which would soon come to an end. Why had Archinard chosen this statuette in particular? Was it a gift? A purchase? A theft? The plate said nothing about any of that, and the statuette remained silent.

The saber was enthroned in another room, the one dedicated to "African appropriations of Abrahamic religions." The scenography of the museum did not mix animist objects with relics of Muslim religious guides. There, too, I identified donations Archinard had made to Le Havre's Museum of Natural History. A horse's saddle, a powder horn, a Koran attributed to Ahmadou. And the tabala presented as "Ahmadou's drum," with its slashed skin.

"You're familiar with the different Muslim brotherhoods, right?"

The room suddenly filled up with dozens of elementary school children on a field trip, accompanied by a guide from the museum.

"Here, we have the Mourides, with Cheikh Ahmadou Bamba," he continued, pointing to the Koranic tablets hanging on the wall. "Those over there are the Layenes."

He turned toward another part of the room.

"You know who the Layenes are, right?"

"Yes," the children replied in unison.

"Good. The Layenes live mainly on the Cape Verde peninsula. And over there, those are the Tijani, with El Hadj Oumar

Tall. In this display case, we have the saber that belonged to Cheikh Oumar."

The swarm of children crowded around the guide, and two boys leaned over the glass.

"Be careful! We do not touch anything!"

A little girl was frenziedly taking photos with her cell phone, of the saber, the drum, the tablets from the Koranic school, desperate for a souvenir of every detail of an unordinary moment. She must have learned her history lesson just as I had thirty-five years before: "... and then he disappeared mysteriously into the caves of Bandiagara."

In the display case, the saber and its sheath were placed side by side, arranged on a stand. "Donation: Louis Archinard, 1909." Curiously, the weapon attributed to the religious guide and jihad leader was a hybrid object. The blade was made in France. The 1821 model said to be "a Montmorency" was used for infantry officers' swords. It still bore the inscriptions "Manufacture de Klingenthal" (Made in Klingenthal) and "Coulaux et Cie" (Coulaux & Co.). The bronze pommel, on the other hand, shaped like a beak, was typical of Toucouleur metallurgy, as was the sheath.

I looked at the saber and thought about the signares of Saint-Louis, about Alfred Amédée Dodds, and the weapons that used to circulate between the French or English merchants and the West African chiefs, Samory, Ahmadou, and El Hadj Oumar Tall. Rather than a symbol of an empire's leader, the weapon seemed more symbolic to me of the intermixing of cultures to which colonial conquest gave rise, whether through collaboration or open conflict, depending on the time and interests of each.

During the restitution ceremony, more than one hundred-fifty years after El Hadj Oumar Tall's death, everyone told their own version of the story. First, Édouard Philippe evoked his own saber, which he had acquired during his military service, then declared that this saber—which was "obviously much more prestigious" than his—indeed belonged "here, in the heart of the Toucouleur Empire, near the people who made it," even though the Toucouleur Empire in question was actually located hundreds of miles away, in what is today Mali and Guinea.

"This saber symbolizes an important chapter in the history of Senegal and its neighboring countries," he went on. "It also symbolizes—including in its warlike qualities—friendship, respect, and the mutual admiration that unites our peoples today."

In the first row of honored guests, sat a range of religious dignitaries, all descendants of El Hadj Oumar Tall, who had come not only from Dakar's mosques, but also from those of Nioro and Ségou in Mali, as well as from Guinea and Nigeria. With their rosaries in hand, in their sumptuously embroidered white, beige and blue boubous and matching chechias, the marabouts did not take much notice of the French Prime Minister in their midst. What was most important was not just that he was present at this event, but rather returning the object, which they hoped would be the first among many. During his speech, the spokesman on behalf of the family, Ahmadou Tall, reminded the audience of what still remained in France, including: "five hundred-eighteen manuscripts, currently housed in France's National Library, a treasure kept at the Quai Branly Museum, Archinard's private collection of objects at the Natural History Museum in Le Havre, one hundred-fifty photographs, which are in Aix-en-Provence, and, finally, a prayer skin and various objects."

Moreover, though they were delighted that the weapon had been returned, the Tall family made clear—this time in Wolof in front of a Senegalese television camera—that this saber did not belong to El Hadj Oumar Tall. It belonged, rather, to his son, Ahmadou, and had been seized from the hands of young Abdoulaye. Again, the version that I had heard in Halwar. Thierno Seydou Nourou Tall, the imam of Dakar's Cheikh Oumar Foutiyou Tall Great Mosque, explained to the camera that Cheikh Oumar's real saber, which was huge, was in the care of his family in Bandiagara, where the guide died in 1864. Regardless of the different versions of the story and their approximations, they in no way affected the solemnity of the moment. Placed on a red cushion with golden fringe, the saber and its sheath passed from the hands of Édouard Philippe to those of President Macky Sall, who in turn presented them to the descendants of the religious guide, who handed them to Hamady Bocoum, director of the Museum of Black Civilizations.

"It was thanks to the prince."

In his spacious office located four floors above the exhibition rooms, Hamady Bocoum recalled the ceremony.

"When the prince decided to do something, he did it," he repeated with a little smile. "I think that all this fuss over restitution is in fashion now. This is a generation that did not experience colonization. Emmanuel Macron's father was not a colonist. Macky Sall did not experience that period of history either. On that day, we took back what belonged to us, but we did it among civilized people."

Since the museum had opened, just after the publication of Savoy-Sarr's report, the director had to take a position on the issue of restitution and on countless occasions, whether fielding questions from European media or invited to speak at conferences abroad. The debate seemed to be more active in Europe than in Senegal.

"The problem," the director went on, "is that we cannot think about African heritage the way Europe would like us to think about it. Here, people do not see them as art objects. Europeans are the ones who turned them into works of art by displaying them in museums."

There was a hint of weariness in his voice.

"Let us decide what to do with those pieces ourselves," he added. "We can burn them, destroy them, or keep them in a museum. Those objects belong to us. It's our decision."

That is what Felwine Sarr, one of the authors of the report commissioned by Emmanuel Macron, seemed to think as well. I met him at his home, in the residential neighborhood of Sacré-Cœur. He came to pick me up in front of the eponymous middle school where a taxi had dropped me off. In his Dakar living room, one full wall of which was covered with books, he told me about his work with Bénédicte Savoy. They spent eight months meeting curators, researchers and jurists, in France and in Africa. And what emerged, he explained, he did not expect: in his words, the "colonial subconscious."

"I knew there were some things that needed to be set straight, that the colonial past and the imagination that was connected to it had not been fully addressed or processed. But then I realized that they hadn't been at all!"

"Meaning?"

"We are often told that we need to move on, not isolate ourselves and become trapped in a painful history. But when we see the violence that emerges with this subconscious, when you start to dig a little..."

"What are you referring to specifically?"

"Arrogance. Some directors of the French museums had the arrogance to think that Africa is incapable of taking care of those objects. And that arrogance along with the conviction that they had done a good thing: that they kept and preserved objects that we would have thought unimportant. When we tell them that those objects are spiritual beings, they look at us with an air of condescension."

He was speaking quickly, stopping sometimes to find a more specific term.

"It's as if it is impossible to for them realize that there is a continent of a billion people with a youth who have the right to their heritage—just like the European youth have the right to their heritage. But no, they think that what is theirs is theirs and what is ours is also theirs! They proclaim the universality of museums, but that universality is self-centered!"

"As if it were impossible to decenter the gaze," I said.

"Exactly. And the same arguments come up again and again: 'But, but there are no museums in Africa'—We have counted around five hundred of them. 'Who should we return them to? Back then, Senegal and Benin didn't even exist.' When the objects had been taken from the Austro-Hungarian Empire, they were returned to Germany or Austria, even though the empire no longer existed. 'The objects were not taken; they were given away or sold.' Yes, given away or sold in an asymmetrical power relationship. Isn't it the same question for Jewish looted property? When Jews sold master paintings for next to nothing in order to escape death, people still returned their property to them or to their descendants. Why don't those analogies work when it comes to us and our heritage?"

I could sense the irritation in his voice. I wondered how many times he had to respond to the same arguments.

"We quickly realize that the question does not play out at the level of reason, but someplace else," he went on. "It has developed as an intimate truth constructed over time, which has been repeated in films, in books, in the media, in history books, and in political speeches. It comes down to the notion that Africans are incapable."

That made me think of the articles written about the jewelry to mark the occasion of their first presentation to the French public in 1893 and the idea that several journalists had advanced: that it could not possibly have been made by Africans.

"And the saber? Why was the saber the first object to be returned?"

"Unlike the violent episodes of dispossession that occurred in Benin and Nigeria, in Senegal, it was different. Here, most objects were stolen during ethnographic missions, and a sort of amnesia set in. Later, the heritage designation focused, for the most part, on relics of saints, such as El Hadj Oumar Tall. I hope that when other requests for restitution are formulated, they will represent all of Senegal's cultural diversity, including the statues from the south of the country, and not only Islamic objects."

He thought for a moment.

"In fact, the restitution of the saber serves as a reminder, not only about the pillaging of objects, but also of the entire historical period of the end of the 19th century. For example, in primary school, we learn that El Hadj Oumar Tall 'disappeared mysteriously in the caves of Bandiagara.' People use the word 'disappeared' instead of saying he was killed, that he was vanquished outright. Today, some people even go as far as to challenge that he even owned a saber because his status as a jihadist figure remains under debate. Some would like to forget that the holy war he waged caused many deaths, whether of the Peul in Macina or the Bambara in Ségou. There is an urgent need for a Senegalese historiography on these questions because when it comes to memory the stakes are high."

I thought back to what Ndiabou Séga Touré had said to me, in the principal's office at the high school in Saint-Louis: "That story about El Hadj Oumar Tall is a sensitive topic." I was beginning to have a deeper understanding of her cautionary tone.

"And what about those who say that the saber is a fake?"

"Mostly, I see it as the complex of the dominated. When you have been defeated, deceived, and cheated, time and time again throughout history, it leaves you with the feeling that you always will be. That distrust can even become a form of intelligence that we claim responsibility for: 'They don't do it to me!' That is our own inconceivability."

Here too, a discourse had been constructed and reinforced over time until it had become truth that everyone had learned to deal with: you can't expect much from white people. When Felwine Sarr's input had been solicited for the report, several of his older African colleagues had expressed doubts.

"They were convinced that nothing would move this time either. I often heard that the mission would be for nothing, that already in the 1970s nothing had come of it. So much failure had been accumulated in the past. When the report was published, the same people shrugged their shoulders: 'Come see me in five years,' people in Dakar would say, 'you'll see. Nothing will happen.'"

"It's as if the relationship to the other could not exist outside of that inconceivability."

"That's right. There is something reassuring about staying with what you know, where everyone knows their place, whether you are white or black. So, I am the one being swindled. And on the other hand, we tell ourselves that we're the ones who know better. And yet, what is interesting in the debate about restitution is precisely that: the symbolic space that it opens, which allows us to reinvent that relationship. Maybe that is the power of those objects.

"Do you think that Emmanuel Macron was aware of that when he made his statement about returning African heritage?"

"I think that, as an individual, he is truly concerned about history. He understands the relationship between memory and history, between what is omitted and what is known as political fact. He understands that France needs Africa to weigh in and play a diplomatic role, and that a different message needs to be sent to the African youth who are demanding other relationships with Europe. Restitution may seem like the solution with the least risk: it maintains economic interests while letting go of the symbolism. The problem is that the symbolism is something we do not control. We are on tectonic plates! As soon as things start moving, it's beyond us. We cannot control that. And that is where he may have been wrong. We cannot play geopolitics with meaning."

I thought about the contracts Édouard Philippe had signed. Obviously, the objective of his visit to Dakar was neither about the saber nor El Hadj Oumar Tall's story, but rather the sale of missiles and three OPV 58 offshore patrol vessels, a transaction worth hundreds of millions of euros. It was as if the saber in that story were but a relic exchanged for influence, like the glassware and other cheap miscellany from colonial times. As if the roles had been determined for so long that it had become impossible to rethink them.

IN THE CAVE

DAKAR, SENEGAL, WITH THE ARCHEOLOGIST ABDOULAYE SOKHNA DIOP

"Don't be afraid," Professor Abdoulaye Sokhna Diop reassured me as he opened his door and noticed my gaze fixed on the empty room with metal props supporting the ceiling. "It was the construction site next door that caused all this damage. We had to reinforce the structure. They're building an eight-story building behind my house, which caused the sand to move beneath my foundation. One day, it was completely bare, between heaven and earth! Well, when we saw that, we thought it was best to just leave. Now, it's just my son and I living here. The rest of the family is staying elsewhere. Come on, let's go into my cave."

The old man walked ahead of me down the corridor, opened a door with a sign written in all caps: "THE CAVE—XUNTT-MI–QUIET!!!" Inside were shelves filled with books and files, a desk on top of which piles of papers overflowed and, small rocks, stones of various colors and sizes all over. Professor Abdoulaye Sokhna Diop was an archeologist, specialized in prehistoric times. He was famous for having thrown a paving stone into Cheikh Oumar Tall's pond, maintaining that, since 1998 and the first journey of the saber, the object had nothing to do with the religious leader. The title appeared on the front page of the daily newspaper, Info 7, on December 17, 1998, in large red letters: "A False History. El Hadj Oumar Tall Never Had a Saber."

Twenty-two years later, at almost eighty years-old, Abdoulaye Sokhna Diop still would not let it go. Sitting there in his office-cave in a residential neighborhood in Dakar, amidst his files and stones, he reflected on what, according to him, was above all a matter of political rivalries.

"It was 1996. We were getting ready for the legislative elections of 1998, and then Abdoulaye Wade, the political opposition at the time, upon his return from one of his trips to Paris, announced that he was planning a surprise for the Senegalese people. He said he was going to bring something back that they did not know about, but which was nevertheless intimately connected to them."

"He used those words?"

"Those were his words! And when he heard it, Mr. Abdou Diouf, then President of the Republic, said to himself: 'Oh! I need to know what that means! Whatever he is hiding, I need to find out!'"

Sitting in his brown plastic chair in front of his library, the professor spoke with gleeful delight as he told the story, playing with silences and intonations, articulating each syllable to better emphasize a word.

"And what did he find out? That it was about a saber that had belonged to El Hadj Oumar and was sitting in some Paris museum. Oh! And then, Mr. Diouf, who had discovered Mr. Wade's secret, got his friend Jacques Chirac going who, in turn, put his sleuths on the case . . . and thus found out that what was referred to as the Ségou treasure was at the Army Museum in Paris."

He paused.

"Well. At the Invalides, there were a bunch of sabers, and he picked out one of them, and called it El Hadj Oumar's saber. And that was that. You know the rest."

"But why are you, personally, interested in this matter?"

"Well, I read in the newspapers that Abdou Diouf was going to have one of El Hadj Oumar's sabers brought here on the eve of the election cycle. It has become quite the story. You know how it is here. A little nugget of information about nothing at all and the press makes it out to be a huge deal, without fact-checking anything. I was convinced that El Hadj Oumar had never even owned a saber that he would have carried with him. Never! So, I wrote that article and submitted it to several newspapers, but all of them snubbed me, except Info 7. They were just starting out back then. The editor-in-chief read the text and wanted to fact-check it. Normal. So, he contacted the director of IFAN, the Museum of African Arts in Dakar, where the saber was to be exhibited, but they did not want to comment. And he is no fool! He said: 'I am the guardian of the saber, and that's all!' Then the editor-in-chief contacted the former minister and Professor Iba der Thiam. He replied that I was not someone to mince words. And that is how it came to be published."

The article in question began with a long preamble, which functioned as much as a warning to the reader as a cover for the author:

> *The reader must be aware of the motives and meaning of the text that he is about to read. He is invited to see only the very ordinary and completely normal desire to help convince the Senegalese people of the cult of truth, especially when it comes to anything that may relate to the materiality of facts belonging to African history in general and Senegalese history in particular.*
>
> *The lines that follow are in no way intended to question the sanctity of Cheikhou Oumar nor that of his actions within the framework of the holy war that he led. I ask, in particular, that the current head of the family of the revered Cheikh in Senegal, Baba Mountaga Tall, to whom the author expresses the deepest respect that he is owed, consider that this article is in no way a denial of the work or actions of the Immortal Cheikh, nor does it minimize one or the other.*

Despite the disclaimers, there was a lot of backlash. By the following day, Info 7 had to publish articles by other researchers who were indignant about the archaeologist's remarks, accusing him of conveying his theories through the press instead of presenting them at scientific colloquia, emphasizing that the saber was above all else a symbol of power and that the religious guide's "real saber" was his pen.

"Still, you knew what you were getting into when you wrote that article?"

"In history, only the facts count," the professor replied. "In 1998, I suggested that those who were challenging me confront me directly. They said: 'The saber exists. Period.' Then they ran away from the debate!"

"What sources did you rely on to prove that that saber was not the one that belonged to El Hadj Oumar Tall?"

"You know, El Hadj Oumar Tall does not have only one family. He has several. There is his family in Dakar and another one in Louga, in Senegal. Then, there are those in Ségou, Nioro, Bandiagara and Koniakary, in Mali. And, lastly, there is his family in Guinea. Do you know about that family in Guinea?"

"Yes, I know there is a Tall family in Guinea."

"Okay. Amongst all those families, all is well . . . except there is no unity. You cannot imagine the tragedies those families have experienced. Un-im-ag-in-able tragedies! I am telling you this, but you need to be very careful. I don't dare tell you what I know, because it could cause problems for you, and for me as well. Well, I can tell you as long as you promise not to record it and not to write it down."

I smiled.

"You know, in my work, I use information that I am given. So..."

"Okay. To use a euphemism: there were many tragic deaths in horrifying situations."

"But how does all that lead to the saber?"

I was feeling a little impatient, and it must have been obvious in my tone. I had just spent days in the archives, and I was hoping for an answer with precise details, not a genealogy of Oumar's family.

"The facts must be put in context," the professor reminded me patiently.

I needed to remember how to listen to stories here. You never interrupted the storyteller.

"So: that saber is linked to El Hadj Oumar Tall," he continued. "Is that a plausible thesis? Back then, sabers were generally gifts. They could be offered by visitors coming to meet the leader of the empire. They could also accompany the purchasing of arms. Okay. We know that El Hadj Oumar was actively fighting between 1850 and 1864. His initial victories posed a threat to the French. He tried to take the fort at Medina, and he besieged it, but Faidherbe, a great tactician, managed to break the siege. After that failure, El Hadj Oumar decided to head northeast, which led him to Ségou."

I concentrated on what he was saying to not interrupt the narrative.

"El Hadj Oumar never once encountered the French on that road. We also know that he never received any French envoys and that he always restocked his weapons in Freetown, in Sierra Leone."

"And therefore, that saber with its French blade..."

"I'm getting to that! I'm getting to that!"

Clearly, I was very undisciplined that day.

"Furthermore, nothing indicates to us that El Hadj Oumar had a saber, I mean: one saber that belonged solely to him and which he carried," the professor went on. "One member of the Oumar family does say that his ancestor had a saber, a big saber, which should be in Bandiagara. He is merely repeating what people in his family have always said. And in fact, that saber does exist, but no one knows where it is. Think about what the Saudis do on Fridays."

The professor stopped for a moment. I waited patiently for the next part of the story, but he indicated that it was my turn to speak.

"Well? What do Saudis do on Fridays?"

"Executions?"

"That's right! Very good! It's a huge saber, like the guillotine! That is the saber he was talking about. But I entirely refute that. I went to Bandiagara, and... there is no saber there."

"Really?"

"No. No saber. Well. Now, there are sabers in what is called the Treasure of Ségou. We also know that El Hadj Oumar Tall's son, Cheikhou Ahmadou, received several French missions. Each one came with their gifts, which could have been sabers. We also know that Ahmadou fought factions of his own family who disobeyed him and that he could have therefore taken sabers from them, sabers which would later be found in Ségou. And then there is the saber that young Abdoulaye held in his hand while defending his mother from Archinard. But nothing proves that the saber returned by Édouard Philippe was that saber either."

As I listened, I saw sabers dancing—in all sizes, from all over. They were evasive, never what they seemed to be. They were constantly escaping from the story we wanted to tell about them, willingly taking refuge in the first theory that was proposed: maybe it was like this, or maybe it was like that.

The professor looked me in the eye and concluded: "Many people are wary of me, because I sit on the rock of truth."

I was sitting on a green plastic armchair facing him, amongst a pile of files, rocks and a map of the ancient Middle East, populated by Hittites, Semites, and Persians, and I felt incapable of guaranteeing anything.

"ALL WE WERE ABLE TO BRING BACK WAS ABDOULAYE"

DAKAR, SENEGAL
AT THE HOME OF
THIERNO MADANI TALL

There were three of us, sitting on the couch facing Caliph Thierno Madani Tall, at his home, in the working-class district of Medina, in Dakar. On my right was Ndiabou Séga Touré, whom I had met in the capital a few weeks earlier. She had asked me if I had ever tried to meet El Hadj Oumar Tall's descendants. I had told her that I wanted to, of course, but I was waiting for the right moment. Then she had suggested that I speak to a friend who knew the family. Two days later, I was meeting Mamadou Samba Mbow, a former journalist at Senegal's public service broadcaster, RTS, then head of the commissioner's office at the General Directorate of Customs. He promised to set up a meeting. It was a done deal. Mamadou Samba Mbow sat down next to Ndiabou. He had just introduced me to the caliph and translated my answer to the question that was posed immediately after we greeted one another: "Why are you, a white woman and descendant of the colonizers, interested in this story?"

The caliph smiled at my answer and began to tell his story.

"The first time that we demanded that France return those objects was in 1993," he began, sitting in a large armchair, in his living room where he usually received the faithful. "It was for the manuscripts." He was with his father then, the late Caliph Thierno Mountaga Tall, whose portrait sat at the back of the room lengthwise, next to a clock indicating the prayer times in red LED lights.

It was early afternoon. The faithful who had gathered for their meal finished eating in the courtyard. Traffic was picking back up in Dakar's crowded streets. The noises of the city were all around us—the bleating sheep, the honking horns, the clinking of the dishes being cleared. Life never stopped in the Medina.

For dozens of years, the caliph recounted, the Tall family paid no attention to the fate of the objects taken from Ségou. All they knew was that young Abdoulaye had died in France at the age of twenty in 1899, after his studies at Saint-Cyr. The family knew nothing about the loot itself until the 1980s. The information had come to them through chance encounters, when the caliph, at the time a student at Al-Azar University in Cairo, was passing through France on vacation and found out from a fellow countryman that some of his ancestor's books were being preserved in the collections of the National Library of France, in Paris.

When he returned to Dakar, without having been able to consult the works in question, he informed his father who at the time was in the middle of writing a biography of that same ancestor, a colossal project which he had been working on for twenty years. The idea of the trip was starting to take root. Who knew? Perhaps those manuscripts contained new information, thoughts of the holy man that did not appear in the books that had escaped the raid and which the family already had.

That was how one day in September of 1993 a delegation of nine people left Medina and its maze of dusty streets for Paris's wide avenues and Rue de Richelieu.

"Mr. Ibrahima Sy, present here, was also on the trip," the caliph said pointing to a tall, thin man sitting in a chair just below the family portrait.

Mr. Sy nodded his head. He had been the father's, then the son's, personal assistant. He was the one who kept the family archives related to this story. I imagined them, wearing elegant Bazin boubous, that shiny damask fabric reserved for outfits for special occasions, white headscarves, lining the passageways lined with the books of France's National Library, consulting one hundred-fifty-year-old works in the manuscript department's reading room—the written Arabic script on yellowed pages, letters traced by their grandfather, the treasure found.

The mission lasted three months. The days were long, especially since the evenings were busy with meetings with the Senegalese religious community in France. Besides, they were the ones who took care of the logistics, the meals, and lodging at 11, Rue Oberkampf, in Paris.

"I still remember the address because I wrote it so many times. At the time there were no emails or SMS messages. We would send letters!" Ibrahima Sy laughed.

Each work was reviewed, based on a catalogue that researchers at the French National Center for Scientific Research (CNRS) had developed in 1985, of which the family was aware.

"Some books gave no new information to Thierno Mountaga since he already had copies of them. He spent more time with others."

In no time the issue of returning the manuscripts came up. The family insisted that they belonged in Dakar, just steps away from the house we were in, at the library of the Cheikh Oumar Tall Mosque, that large mosque with its four towers topped with green balls, which was visible from the Route de la Corniche that stretched along the coast, overlooking the Atlantic. However, for the French authorities, there was no question: according to the law, the books were part of French heritage and were therefore their inalienable property. Once they were entered into a French institution's inventory, they could no longer be removed. That was the law. Period. The fact that the objects had been taken by force—in other words stolen—changed absolutely nothing. Of course, there was an exception in the law which concerned illicitly acquired objects, but the irony of history was that it did not apply to the objects from Ségou: they were spoils of war, taken as spoils, a practice that was perfectly authorized and regulated by law, banned only in 1899 by the Hague Convention (though France would never apply that in its colonies). In 1890, Archinard was thus within his rights. France responded with a bar to proceedings, without the possibility of appeal.

"So, we decided to proceed otherwise," the caliph explained. "We put everything on microfilm."

The operation was entirely financed by the religious adherents residing in France, who contributed a sum of one hundred thousand French francs invoiced by the French National Library (BNF) for the microfilm, as well as for buying a machine to consult them. Couldn't all that have been done free of charge?

"Such a request would have required official measures on the part of the State of Senegal," Ibrahima Sy explained. "For the family, the important thing was to reaffirm its right to those objects. To say that they were not giving up on getting them back."

The caliph interrupted the conversation and excused himself: he was going to receive a devotee. We could stay, he told us, and we would resume the discussion afterwards. Two men entered, knelt on the floor at the foot of the armchair in which their guide was sitting, and whispered their reason for coming. With one hand placed on their shoulder, the caliph listened and recited a prayer. The room was suddenly completely silent. Outside, in the courtyard, the meal had ended. I could hear the clinking of the cutlery that had just been washed, and the sound of the water rinsing the white tin basins. Then, once they had expressed their gratitude through words and gestures, the men left looking relieved. We could resume our conversation.

"All that we could bring back from France was Abdoulaye," the caliph continued.

During their stay, the delegation learned that the remains of El Hadj Oumar Tall's grandson, who was buried at the Montparnasse cemetery, would soon be exhumed and cremated, as was done for all expiring burial plot concessions. The idea was unacceptable, particularly since the Muslim religion prohibits cremation. The caliph recalled the words of his father: "That man was not made for fire."

The body was repatriated two years later, in 1995, the time it took for official measures to be taken, which this time involved the State of Senegal. Abdoulaye's body returned with military honors in a plane provided by the French army, accompanied by military personnel from Saint-Cyr. There was a tribute to him at the Invalides, followed by another—this time to the general staff of the Senegalese army—upon his arrival in Dakar. The funerary ceremony took place in the Oumar family mosque, then the body was brought to Ségou.

Having left his native land with colonial troops more

than one hundred years earlier, Abdoulaye had returned as a member of the military, celebrated by two armies. As I sat in the caliph's living room, I could not help but think that there was something odd about that image. I thought about the harshness of the words I had read in the archives—about chiefs' sons, about Archinard's plan to cut all ties between those children and the communities they came from and send them to France to guarantee their loyalty to the colonial power.

"Look, that's him," Ibrahima Sy said to me, handing me his telephone. Displayed on the screen was a portrait of a young man in a military uniform. The following photo showed the same man in a traditional boubou. "Abdoulaye was the first Black person to attend Saint-Cyr," the assistant added. There was pride in his voice. All the complexity of such a common story was undoubtedly there: the same achievement could be seen at once as a symbol of defeat and success.

"And what about the jewelry? Have you found any information about the jewelry in your research?" Ibrahima Sy asked.

"The jewelry is on reserve at the Quai Branly Museum," I said. "It is not on display. I was not able to see it. I was only able to consult the archives."

"Is there anything about gold in the archives?"

"No, just jewelry, some of which is gold, some is silver."

"I'm thinking about gold. We've heard about gold bars."

"We are not interested in the gold," the caliph interrupted.

"Right, he says he doesn't care about it, but I do!" Ibrahima Sy replied with a chuckle.

"All we are interested in are the manuscripts and Abdoulaye," the caliph concluded.

When his father died, the son took over the research. In 2011, it led him to Le Havre, to follow Archinard's path.

"We asked a Senegalese man living in Le Havre to help us," the caliph explained. He was talking about Mamadou Ly, a former senator for Senegalese living abroad. He was the one who had established the connection with the Natural History Museum and then museum director Cédric Crémière.

"There were many objects, not all of them from Ségou. Some, you could see, had been taken from people's private lives. A comb, for example," Ibrahima Sy recalled.

The caliph also found himself looking at horse saddles, gaiters, spears, a Koran, the three-legged tabala from Ouéssébougou, as well as statuettes and masks from Bamana culture—all of which I had seen at the Museum of Black Civilizations.

"When we saw what was in those boxes, we thought: we need to show that to people," said Ibrahima Sy.

A one-day ephemeral exhibition was organized at Le Havre's city hall, the mayor of which was no other than Édouard Philippe. The organizers on the French side expected to receive about fifty visitors. Five hundred people arrived by bus from all over France. The phantom objects on reserve came back to life to the astonishment of the mayor and the Natural History Museum director. A dozen of those pieces would be exhibited in Dakar three years later, for the Ziarra, an annual pilgrimage around commemorating El Hadj Oumar Tall.

"That day, in Le Havre, I said something to Édouard Philippe," the caliph recalled, half smiling. "I told him that one day those objects would come back to their rightful owner, and I invited him to Senegal."

"The caliph prayed for him, and he became Prime Minister. It was his fate" Ibrahima Sy added.

Ibrahima Sy recalled the emotion of that day at the ceremony marking the saber's restitution when among the honored guests, they were both there.

"For us, that saber which came back is symbolic of Cheikh Oumar. That is how significant it is for us. And I think it was also important for Archinard since he took it with him to France."

"What do you think about those who say that it wasn't the guide's real saber?"

"That is a futile and useless debate," Ibrahima Sy maintained. "First of all, we never said that Cheikh Oumar had only one saber. He could have had several. Secondly, if that saber held no symbolic or military interest, why would Archinard hold on to it?"

Caliph Thierno Madani did not say much. Perhaps he did not really want to bring up that warlike symbol in the middle of our conversation. Talking about jihad was a delicate affair.

Things can rapidly conflate, and it is a slippery slope. Besides, the caliph explained, El Hadj Oumar Tall did not plan to fight the French.

"But when you are attacked, you defend yourself. We did not invite the French to our land. They intruded upon us. Cheikh Oumar led a holy war, but he did not initially plan to do that."

Our discussion was coming to an end. It had gone on longer than expected, and now it was time to go.

"So, what is the next step of your project?" the caliph asked me.

"I am going to come back to see you again. I don't know when yet, but I will come back."

"Very well. You have knocked on the right door. We will help you. And may God help you with this project."

OBJECTS OF DEVOTION

LE HAVRE, FRANCE
NATURAL HISTORY MUSEUM

The three-legged drum with a hole was lying on its side, placed on bubble wrap, spread out on a table with wheels. On another table was the antelope crest, the Ndomo mask, and a horse saddle. All the pieces that I had seen in Dakar one year prior on exhibit at the Museum of Black Civilizations were now back in Le Havre. The next part of my research would be conducted in France, starting here, in Archinard's birth city.

The three women I was with had grabbed their fleece jackets before heading inside. Anne Liénard, the director of Le Havre's Natural History Museum, Gabrielle Baglione, curator, and Awa Ndiaye Samb, the Department Head at the Museum of Black Civilizations, were well aware of how cool the temperature was in the reserves. For one week now, they had been working on the "Archinard collection," which consisted of more than ninety objects from Toucouleur or Bambara culture, of Muslim or Animist inspiration, as well as some objects from Congo and Gabon, all of which were donations that the officer had made to the city.

Anne Liénard opened a drawer in which knives, daggers, and powder horns were arranged. In the one beneath it, a comb. I remembered the emotion in Ibrahima Sy's voice in Dakar: "objects taken from people's intimate lives." Sometimes a simple everyday object conceals violence. Next to that, a photograph: two women, one sitting on a barrel, the other on the floor in front of her. The former was running a comb like the one in the drawer through the latter's hair. As if the photo were the caption that went with the object.

In the third drawer, laid out on bubble wrap, were several wooden statuettes, including the "little favorite," which I had seen in Dakar.

"It looks like they're asleep," I said.

"Or maybe they're not," Awa Ndiaye Samb replied.

I smiled: "It's true. We don't know."

It has been ten years already since the caliph had come to visit the Natural History Museum, but Gabrielle Baglione still remembered. At the time, the reserve was not located outside of Le Havre. It was at the fort in Tourneville, on top of a hill, where the municipal archives were now kept. From the fort, we had a breathtaking view of the lower part of the city, the sea, the port, and the city center. It was July 2011. The Museum was expecting only three people, but to their surprise a delegation of twenty-seven Senegalese people walked through the door, all decked out in flowing Bazin boubous.

In one of the photos taken on that occasion, we saw them all gathered around four tables, which were arranged together as if forming an island, covered with plastic crates that were filled with objects. A powder horn, a leather saddlebag and warriors' caps. Daggers, arrows and spear tips. And the comb. Caliph Thierno Madani Tall was seated on a chair wearing black glasses, holding a rosary in his hand, fascinated by the objects he was seeing for the first time. A young man was filming with a camcorder from the other side of the table. Everyone looked serious. Something very solemn was captured when that photo had been taken. Gabrielle Baglione was at the back of the room, off to the side, observing the scene as if she were not part of it. Neither she nor Cédric Crémière, the director of the Natural History Museum at the time, had anticipated the fervor of the moment. The latter explained to me that prior to that visit he was completely unaware of the importance of what the museum had in its reserves.

"That day we realized that those objects were laden with meaning," Gabrielle Baglione explained to me. "We understood that simply imagining that those objects were perhaps connected to such-and-such a figure made them come alive, made them powerful. It did not matter if that connection were proven or not."

"You mean, even whether or not those objects belonged to the Tall family history?"

"That's right. And we did not expect it to be the case. We are museum people. Our job is to ensure that those objects be maintained in good condition and to conserve them—not to have an emotional or human connection with them. That is out of our purview! And then, we realized that..."

She was searching for the right words.

"We realized that, between guaranteeing the origin of the object and how we could appraise it, the object could have two statuses. And both statuses were legitimate. That is truly what I felt that day."

"Some visitors may feel that the object is still sacred," Awa Ndiaye Samb added. "We also see that in our museum."

"That's right. Of course, we know that the museum status of an object is not a status in absolute terms. Half of museum collections are made up of sacred objects. All we noticed was that those objects, which had been conserved thanks to our efforts, elicited emotion in those who were so inclined. In some way, that also justified our conservation work. Besides, people often thanked us for preserving them."

When the objects were placed on display at Le Havre's town hall a few days later, the crowd that came to see them exhibited the same devotion. In fact, there were so many people that neither Caliph Thierno Madani nor Mayor Édouard Philippe were able to deliver a speech for the visitors.

"Nobody would listen," Gabrielle Baglione recalled. "They had to make their official speeches in the mayor's office. Look at this."

The curator showed me some photos on her computer. First, the positioning of the dozen objects on display, placed on a large table covered with a white tablecloth, which sat in the middle of a huge exhibition hall: the drum, the comb, a powder horn, a whip, a riding whip, a wooden lock, a leather satchel, two quivers and some arrows, a boubou, some warrior headdresses, the antelope crest, and the "little favorite." It was their first public appearance since the 1980s. In one display case documents retraced Archinard's story and placed next to the table was his flag.

The first visitors were women and children of all ages, from little ones in strollers to teenagers, all gathered around the roped-off area around the table. Their gazes fixed on what was placed on top, they took their cell phones out of their pockets and handbags to immortalize the objects.

The space was filling up. More women—older women—arrived, one leaning on her cane. Then some men joined them. Everyone was wearing Senegalese clothing—blue, yellow, red, orange, and mauve ensembles, which added color to the room. They all pointed their cell phones at the warrior's boubou, the drum, the arrows, pushing against the rope barriers a little more to be able to get a little closer. Strollers were parked in one corner; the children sat on the wooden floor. In front of the table of objects, a little girl wearing a pink Hello Kitty cap and a yellow dress made from the same Bazin fabric as her mother's boubou, fiddled with the rope barrier, looking a little lost amidst an increasingly dense crowd—so dense that there seemed to be no more space in that room that had appeared so huge a few hours earlier.

Four teenage girls sat along the edge of a large window trimmed with heavy red velvet curtains. Behind them were the fountains of City Hall square, buildings with rectilinear layouts, built after the war, and the French flag fluttering in the wind. Those folks are the current residents of Le Havre, heirs at once to Fouta's heroes as well as the city's soldiers. Their gazes were staring directly into the camera. That was when the caliph arrived, wearing a white boubou with a green scarf.

The level of intensity went up a notch as the dignitary walked toward the table, a TV camera following him. The barrier fell, and people were now glued to the table, their hands extended in an attempt to touch one of the bag's leather straps, straps or lift an edge of the warrior's boubou, gazing upon the trace of a glorious past that had traveled through time.

"It was very unsettling," said Gabrielle Baglione. "Everyone wanted to touch the objects."

"Everyone wanted *barkeelu*," Awa Ndiaye smiled. "It was like that with the saber too. After the restitution ceremony at the presidential palace in Dakar, we had a lot of trouble getting it out of there. Everyone wanted to touch it."

"Yes, it was religious fervor. It had gone beyond simply memorializing it. We sensed their need to appropriate part of that history. It was beyond all of us."

In the next photo, the table was empty. We found the objects in the mayor's office, placed on a low table, surrounded by the elected official, the caliph and his delegation. That is where the speeches were made, in a small group. When they opened their palms toward the sky for a prayer led by the caliph, Édouard Philippe looked disoriented wearing his suit and tie amidst all those flamboyant boubous.

Then the visitors left. In the last photo, the objects were once again by themselves, laid out on the coffee table of a deserted room, except that in the background, near the door through which one last piece of boubou has just disappeared, was a group of five white people whose eyes were glued to the table, looking amazed.

Mamadou Ly was with the caliph that day. A resident of Le Havre since 1976, he was originally from Fouta, or, more precisely, Donaye, about twenty miles from Halwar. Ciré Harouna Ly, who was with me in the village where El Hadj Oumar Tall was born, was his nephew. Mamadou Ly was the one that Caliph Thierno Madani called upon to help him prepare his visit to Le Havre.

"This is all a happy coincidence. Perhaps it is destiny, who knows?" he said.

His family had close ties with the Tall family: his uncle Souleymane Wone was Thierno Seydou Nourou Tall's right hand man, Thierno Madani's great uncle and an emblematic figure of the Tijani brotherhood.

"When I left Senegal to study in France, the last person I saw in Dakar was Thierno Seydou Nourou Tall. I took my bags, and on my way to the airport I stopped at his place with my uncle so that he could give me a blessing. So, sometimes I think that he entrusted me with that mission!"

Forty-five years later, that coincidence still brought a smile to Mamadou Ly's face. After all, he wasn't supposed to have stayed in Le Havre. He had been trying to get to Paris, but finding a place to live in the capital proved difficult and he had ended up in Normandy where friends of his parents took him in initially, where he completed his studies between Le Havre, Rouen and Caen.

"Then I got married and settled down permanently in Le Havre. Now I've been here quite a while, but I will always remember the day I arrived. It was July 29, 1976, a sweltering summer day. With that sun that never sets! Having a day last so long was at once surprising and impressive."

Another detail had surprised Mamadou Ly: the people of Le Havre did not know who Louis Archinard was. For him, who had studied history in high school in Dakar, it was inconceivable that in the city where the general was born, no one remembered the man who had "made the French Sudan." So, when he arrived there, he told himself that he would search the city for traces of Archinard—starting with the avenue that was named after him, just two steps away from the Senegalese consulate where we were standing.

Mamadou Ly was a regular there. He was heavily involved in the life of Le Havre's Senegalese community, "about 10,000 people," he specified, a community which was formed around the automobile industry, in particular the Renault factories which were recruiting in the Senegal River region. In the workers' residential quarters, men formed groups based on the villages they came from, pooling their resources to help build a school, a health center, and a new well back home. That solidarity allowed several localities in Fouta to guarantee potable water, education and healthcare to their residents.

"A few days after I arrived in Le Havre, I decided to visit the city. As I sat on a bench in the square, which is now the Oscar Niemeyer Cultural Center, an African man started speaking to me in Pulaar. As we talked, I learned that he came from the same region I did. He invited me to his boarding house, an on-site residential area for immigrant workers, many of whose inhabitants were from Fouta. A lot of them did not know how to read or write because in their village there was no school. That is how they ended up working at the Renault factory and I a student at the university. After I met him, I got involved with the boarding house."

The first action the young student took was to offer free literacy courses so that his compatriots no longer had to ask for help to write letters to their families. Later, when he began teaching economics and management courses, Mamadou Ly organized the High Council of Senegalese Abroad of Le Havre, which hosted cultural events and working groups for employment, housing, and security. In 1999, he was even elected senator of the Senegalese Living Abroad, a position he held for two years, until the Senate was dissolved.

Yet, even with that strong historical connection, even with

the presence of a sizable Senegalese community, Mamadou Ly was not familiar with the Natural History Museum's objects and nor was his community. It was Caliph Thierno Madani who told him they existed, he himself having obtained information about them from a certain Roland Colin, a researcher and former Senegalese government advisor at the very beginning of independence.

"Mr. Colin knew that there were objects in Paris's museums, but that there were also some in Le Havre. That is why the caliph contacted me and asked if I could help him to prepare a visit," Mamadou Ly said.

When he called the Natural History Museum in Le Havre, he realized that nobody had a clear idea of what was in the reserve. It was as if those pieces had fallen into oblivion the moment they were removed from their display cases.

He had a perfectly clear memory of the reaction of the members of the delegation when the crates were finally opened: "People were in tears. The symbolism of it was so strong, it was almost irrational. We want to be close to those objects not because of history, but because we feel a spiritual connection to them."

It was as if that day, in the reserves, then later, on the day of the exhibition at city hall, some arrows, a drum, and a warrior's cap had revealed the relationship between Le Havre and the river valley. As if the Senegalese presence in that city had suddenly taken on a historical significance that surpassed any one individual's decision to emigrate.

Mamadou Ly interrupted my thoughts.

"Today, our youth are not familiar with how we practice our religion. Senegalese Islam is not a political Islam. It is an Islam of peace and prayer. However, what I have seen for some time now, when I go to the mosque, worries me. Boys are dressing like Salafis, and girls are increasingly wearing the veil. Those influences are not part of our religious traditions. It's too bad."

He sounded irritated and concerned.

"More recently, when I was teaching at the high school," he added, "I was the only teacher who dared to address the question of religion with the youth because I knew what I was talking about. I had a solid religious education, and I studied Arabic as a second language in high school in Dakar. One of my teachers was a French national whose specialization was Arabic. During religious festivals, he used to give lectures that were based on the Koran, then he would invite debate. It was very informative."

"Isn't there also a need for the youth to construct their identity by turning to an Islam that is more visible, by wearing the veil, for example?" I asked him.

"The problem in France is the banalizing discourse that the Le Pen family has trivialized. For over forty years that family—first the father, and now the daughter and the niece—has been creating a terminology of exclusion which has permeated French society. People repeat that discourse with no awareness of its impact. Young people experience that every day.

They are told that they are not fully French because they come from elsewhere. In my discussions with them at the high school, I used to tell them: 'France is your country. Be proud that you are French. Senegal is also your country, but you are not very familiar with it. It is an emotional connection.' They would reply to me saying that here people did not see them as French. And I would say to them: 'Know who you are and be confident about it! You do not need to wait for someone to realize that you and they have the same rights. Just know who you are. No one is going to do that for you.'"

Mamadou Ly stopped for a moment.

"The problem is that the families of those young people have fewer networks than the others in a world where everything revolves around networks, whether it's finding an internship, a job or a place to live. Because of research that leads absolutely nowhere, young people feel excluded, and marginality becomes very tempting. Some go through the prison pipe, which makes integration even more difficult. That is very fertile territory for Islamists. We wanted to fight it by creating the Senegalese High Council of Le Havre. We wanted to promote social integration of the community by allowing everyone to take ownership of their city and country. We were accused of communitarianism, but we persevered. Education, employment and housing are guarantees for a stable life."

Mamadou Ly's smile was bleak.

"And what about Archinard? Are you still interested in his story?

"Yes. General Archinard symbolizes our shared history. The Archinard collection illustrates the connection between our histories, that of the former French Sudan and that of France, with Le Havre at its epicenter. I am interested in him as a figure, even if it is painful for me to dig up that history. France, along with several other European countries, grew their wealth for several centuries, first from the slave trade and then from colonial occupation, both of which produced the effects we are well aware of today. The conquest and domination of other peoples is part of human nature. Although a victim of it today, at one point in her history, Africa did the same thing."

Then Mamadou Ly asked me if I had been to Archinard's tomb in the city's heights, next to Fort Tourneville and the municipal archives.

"Naba Kamara, a child whom he had brought back from Africa and who lived in Le Havre until she died, is also at rest in the family vault. She lived with Archinard's sister. A few days before Thierno Madani Tall's visit, the municipal services had the tomb cleaned at my request."

So Abdoulaye was not the only child brought to France by the colonial troops' commander.

"And who was Naba Kamara?"

"She was the daughter of Djémé Kamara, a Bambara warrior and one of Archinard's companions in arms who fought against the Oumar family. Do you see the ambiguity of the Le Havre conqueror? On the one hand, he was the strong arm of colonial conquest, and on the other a father to Abdoulaye, affectionately referred to in Le Havre as "the Eaglet", the nickname of Napoleon's son. He was also a father figure for Naba Kamara, who dressed like the women of Le Havre, as I saw in a photo of her with Archinard. She seemed quite integrated."

THE CITY WITH NO HISTORY

LE HAVRE, FRANCE
MUNICIPAL ARCHIVES

The *Visitor's Pocket Illustrated Guide* to Le Havre's Museum of Natural History dates to 1904. The city's municipal archives still have a copy. I opened the blue cover with gold lettering, leafed through the first pages, and read: "In 1892, the number of visitors, on the days the museum is open was 34,720. In 1902, 33,935. School children often visit the museum with their teachers. The rooms are open to them, at the director's request, on days that the museum is not open to the public."

That's a lot of people, I thought, for a city like Le Havre whose population at that time was about 115,000. I looked at the photo boards illustrating each room—the paleontology room on the ground floor, photos of mammals, zoology and anatomy on the first floor, and lastly, the brand-new ethnography and prehistory room on the second floor, inaugurated three years earlier, which housed "the considerably rich recently acquired collection." I imagined the people of

Le Havre at the beginning of the previous century wandering around peering into the display cases exhibiting stuffed animals, butterfly and fossil collections and, on the top floor, arrows and quivers, straw hats and ivory bracelets, verses from the Koran and fertility fetishes.

I noticed Archinard's name, logged as a donor, in several parts of the guide. My search was like a treasure hunt—sometimes looking for the trace of an object in military documents that were over 130 years old, and other times trying to find the name of the military man in the museum's inventory. During that visit to Le Havre's municipal archives, I was focused on the latter.

Next to the *Visitor's Pocket Illustrated Guide*, a stack of papers sat there waiting for me. It was bundle no.9 of box no. 4, the one that contained all the documents connected to the Natural History Museum, in other words 19 bundles in all—namely what had escaped the Allied bombardments and displacements. If you wanted to know more about the history of the collections, you had to rummage through the place. At the museum itself, destroyed then rebuilt, only scattered papers remained, collected in a cardboard file box that Anne Liénard, the director, and Awa Ndiaye, who had come from Dakar, had been combing through when I met them. In Le Havre, for anyone who was interested in the city's history, the memory of war and its traces were constantly evoked.

"We still have a few boxes of archives whose contents are unknown," Gabrielle Baglione told me when we reached the archives room. "Until we open them to look at what is inside, there's always the hope of finding something."

The pile was made up of letters concerning private donations to the Museum between 1885 and 1903. They were sometimes politely refused, as was this sailor's uniform proposed by a certain Louis Journaux, to whom the mayor wrote:

> *In its meeting of December 8, 1886, the municipal council expressed the wish to only admit [to the museum] curiosities exhibiting a marked antique or exotic character, and it must be noted that despite its incontestable interest, the object you have offered fits neither one nor the other of those categories.*

Ethnographic objects made up only part of the donations at the Natural History Museum, which mainly received stuffed birds, shell collections and paleontology publications. But at the end of the 19th century, curiosities that came from afar were increasingly common. Le Havre was a port city where countless merchants were making a fortune off the colonies. And then there were the members of the military, like Archinard, who would regularly give away objects they had collected on the battlefields. His very first gift dated to August 3, 1889, eight months before Ségou was sieged. Among the thirty objects were hairpins, fishing nets, and fishhooks, but also "the boubou of a warrior who was killed in Koundian"; "the hat of a warrior killed in Oulada"; and "a fabric hat, gleaned from the combat zone in Koundian."

I thought about the boubou I had seen in the Natural History Museum's reserves, with stains that were still visible on the woven fabric. "Blood stains," Awa Ndiaye had thought. I wondered who had been responsible for undressing the fallen warrior to retrieve that boubou and hat.

"Allow me to express my sincere thanks," the mayor wrote to Archinard, "for your generous gift of these very curious objects, which are a great enrichment to the major scientific institution of our city."

Two years later, regarding the second gift from the officer, his gratitude was even more emphatic:

"Allow me, Colonel, to express my sincere thanks, on behalf of the municipal administration, for your generous gift whose provenance is particularly dear to us, and please accept, once again, our most distinguished regards."

It was August 14, 1891, one year after the siege of Ségou. The Natural History Museum's curator, Gustave Lennier, noted in his inventory log: "a black dancer's costume from Upper Senegal, two hats, a quiver and 50 arrows, a powder horn, a musical instrument, a sort of harmonica made out of wood and string."

No trace of the objects taken in Ségou—they had been sent to Paris where they would later be exhibited. Those latter objects were from Archinard's personal collections. Other donors followed suit. One Mr. Thierry, who lived at rue Garibaldi, donated a large quantity of objects from Dahomey on October 8, 1901, including a pair of sandals, a white hammock, animal hides, and a knife. On June 16, 1902, Mr. G. Lefèbre gave objects from Haiti. In July 1902, Mr. Millot gifted objects from Congo, Guinea, Gabon, Senegal, and from Upper Ubangi. And in 1908, one Mr. Lucas, a lieutenant in the colonial infantry, gave the gift of a "superb [the word is underlined three times] ethnographic collection of objects from Upper Senegal and Upper Niger." The museum director advised the mayor: "You should send a letter of thanks to number 30, Boulevard Maritime, Le Havre, expressing our sincere gratitude that is proportionate to the great interest of the collection that has been so generously gifted."

I went from one letter to the next, seeing how the Natural History Museum built its collection of insects, hummingbirds, shells, crocodile heads, hats, an albatross, a palm leaf with bird nests, a seal, a marten from Guyana, a monkey, fish, a gorilla skull from Gabon, and another skull, this time of a royal tiger from Cochinchina. Then, in the next letter in the pile: "a skull of a Neo-Caledonian and ten skulls of Peruvians" gifted by Dr. Hamy, the Natural History Museum's director. Suddenly I wondered how many human skulls were conserved in France's natural history museums.

During those years, Archinard was a famous figure in Le Havre. In August of 1891, one year after the siege of Ségou, when he had just made his second donation to the Natural History Museum, the city's Society of Commercial Geography had organized a banquet in his honor. The event, which was featured in the former daily newspaper Le Petit Havre, which I consulted on microfilm, brought together 130 guests in the Frascati room, with a "view of the hotel terrace and of the sea." Toasts were made to "the child from Le Havre, who had so gloriously carried and waved the French flag so far away over the Sudan." The menu, which consisted of ten courses followed by "fruits and desserts," was served with champagne and wine as Archinard's exploits were recalled with considerable detail in the speeches celebrating the commanding officer's bravery. To highlight Archinard's conquests, which were presented as "fruitful endeavors not only for us, but also for the native populations who suffer the yoke of fanatic warriors who are their leaders," Ahmadou, Samory, and Mamadou Lamine's were evoked. Anybody who was anybody in the city seemed to be there, from the mayor to the president of the Chamber of Commerce, including the chief of the Marine Services. The journalist recounted the applause, commenting in passing on the speeches "where the purest patriotic breath mingles so intimately, in its contained form, with the praise of Lieutenant-Colonel Archinard."

Then it was the hero of the evening's turn to speak. Archinard told the story of his conquests with false modesty: "What I did over there is what anyone else would have done." He criticized Paris's reluctance to engage in armed combat, for financial reasons:

> *The instructions were quite dangerous. It was a bit like telling a ship captain today: we wanted to make a boat, but that is very costly. Perhaps we will change our minds. In the meantime, half of it is made. Start navigating with that and we will see how you do and whether we need to eventually complete it.*

Given that the siege of Ségou had been commented on extensively by the preceding orators, Archinard was content to discuss budgetary matters of military expeditions. He concluded with a remark about Abdoulaye:

> *I have finished speaking, but I would like to add a word about the little prince Abdoulaye, that handsome and intelligent child people are constantly going on about to me, who I brought back last year because, the governor and I agreed that, from a religious point of view, his presence in the Sudan as well as in Senegal was troubling.*
>
> *He does not belong to me, as you know. Yet if he is fond of me, it is because I have treated him well, just as I have treated all the prisoners well. I have released him to the Under Secretary of State, and it is the government who had him and who has him now.*

I reread the passage, an odd mix of affection and distance. What exactly were people "constantly" saying to him about Abdoulaye? Was it to express their surprise that a French colonel would bring back an enemy's son? Was he being accused of being too close to him? Or was it simple curiosity tinged with exoticism? One thing seemed certain: the group of Le Havre guests who had been invited to that dinner was perfectly aware of the "little prince's" existence and had an opinion on the matter—and Archinard seemed to want to set the record straight.

A little over half a mile from the Natural History Museum, in his house looking over the city, historian Claude Malon returned to the paternal image that Archinard projected in Le Havre. He spoke to me about an old woman from Le Havre who, in the late 1990s, still remembered "Archinard's Negress" strolling around the city, wearing beautiful dresses. It was Naba Kamara.

Married late in life, Archinard did not have any children with his wife. But there was Abdoulaye, with the bizarre status of "well-treated prisoner," fond of the one who had kidnapped him then returned him to the government. And there was also Naba, who had arrived in France when she was a little girl, about seven or eight years-old, and was raised by Archinard's sister.

"Archinard was one of those rare figures in Le Havre who actually went there, to Africa. Le Havre's connection to the colonies was very strong, because of the port, but most merchants never went there themselves. That explains why people do not generally identify Le Havre as a colonial port, like Bordeaux or Marseille, for instance," Claude Malon pointed out. Besides, when he had begun his research in the 1990s, there was nothing about Le Havre's colonial time, as if that period of the city's history had never existed. He had wanted to study it through the lens of the economy, "because without the economy, you cannot get to the heart of the matter." He explained that the history of Le Havre's companies did not follow the same trajectory as that of other colonial ports.

"You have to go back to the period of the slave trade. The companies based in Le Havre traded mostly with Saint-Domingue and therefore, at the end of the slave trade, they did not redeploy into the colonies. Other traders from Le Havre had financial interests, but no possessions. It was what was referred to at the time as 'local businesses,' not to be confused with 'colonial businesses' such as those in Bordeaux and Marseille. The people of Le Havre worked with agents, men they trusted, who would secure goods, like coffee, cacao and exotic wood. They made use of commercial advantages established by the relationship of colonial domination, without investing in possessions."

That was the world Archinard had entered: a city where the economic stakes connected to the colonies were high, but where few had any personal ties. There was room for the construction of narratives, for the imagination to run free—with little competition.

"There were political figures who were more discrete too, like Gilbert Vieillard," said Claude Malon. "Gilbert Vieillard was a colonial administrator who was very critical of its hierarchy, who had learned Pulaar, wore African dress and became friends with Amadou Hampaté Bâ, a great Malian author. But in the Le Havre of the early-20th century, he was not so prominent.

"Colonization is about those two figures: the conqueror and the mediator," Claude Malon insisted. "Even if I must admit that I have a personal preference for the latter! I do not believe that colonization played a positive role, which the law of 2005* argues, but I also do not believe in repentance. Rather, I believe in trying to be objective in my work as an historian."

I asked him how he would explain the fact that there remains such little trace of all that history in the collective memory of the people of Le Havre.

"The imagination is a very effective tool, but it can quickly be replaced by another idea. In the case of Le Havre, the war and the bombardments of 1944 eclipsed everything that had happened previously. The city had been razed, people were dying of hunger and had no roofs over their heads. Reconstruction consumed everything. That trauma even managed to mask the period of collaboration that had preceded it—in this case, *a fortiori*, the colonial period! All the pre-war proselytizing efforts disappeared discretely.

"So, how exactly did the traders fare?"

"Very well. They saw an opportunity for profit. They said to themselves: what if we were not so colonial? They were excellent at securing goods and, besides, they did not have to worry about the problems they would have had with possessions in Madagascar or Senegal. So, in the 1960s, when colonialism had gone afoul and become obsolete, they established privileged relationships with the new independent States quite easily. If you go through the records of the Chamber of Commerce, you can see quite clearly how their discourse evolved."

Archinard did not live to see the tides turn. He died before then. In 1929, at the age of 79, knowing he was nearing the end of his life, he made a third donation to The Natural History Museum of Le Havre, including the tabala from Ouéssébougou and the "little favorite," objects that had remained at his home for forty years. That time, his gesture was staged: Archinard insisted that he be the one to place the drum in the display case, which from that point onward would be dedicated to his donations.

Later, the Natural History Museum published a brochure featuring "Archinard's collection," in which then curator, Adrien Loir, recalled the general's emotion at the inauguration and the story he had told about the siege of Ouéssébougou:

"We had been fighting there nonstop for two days," the general said to me. "The persistent, cadenced, monotonous sound of the war drum accompanied our every movement, but, in the end, we had them trapped. They jumped over the walls into the interior courtyards as they beat down the door with their blows. Then, it all burst into flames. Chief Bandiougou-Diara had just gotten blown up along with his people, and the drum stopped beating."

Until the very end of his life, Archinard had cultivated his own African legend. And yet, by the end of 1893, only two years after the siege of Ségou, he was relieved of his duties as troop commander. Having returned to France to seek medical attention, he learned a few months later before he was to go back, that the French Sudan was now administered by civilians, no longer by the military. He continued to move up in the ranks, but never again set foot in Africa to command troops.

When Archinard died in 1932, his funeral drew a sizeable crowd to Le Havre. The media published long biographies, where the sieges of Ségou and Ouéssébougou figured as key moments not only of the general's career, but also of France's advancement in West Africa.

Among the troops that accompanied the general's casket from the temple to the Sainte-Marie Cemetery, was a row of Senegalese riflemen. In the photos conserved in the municipal archives, they often appeared blurry in the foreground, or at the edge of the frame, as if they were part of the setting rather than characters in their own right.

Two years later, the City of Le Havre erected a statue to honor the general with the inscription: "To General Louis Archinard, 1850-1932, peacemaker and colonizer of the French Sudan." The monument was identical to the one that was inaugurated in Ségou in December of 1933. At the end of World War II, the Le Havre statue was nowhere to be found. Made of bronze, it had been melted down during German occupation. War and occupation had completely erased any memory or physical trace of the colonial period—including at The Natural History Museum, which had also been completely destroyed by a fire following the bombardments in 1944. Of the ethnographic collections, all that remains today is what had been stored in six crates by the young curator at the time, André Maury, six crates sheltered in the safety of the Graville priory in January 1942. In the papers that Anne Liénard, Gabrielle Baglione and Awa Ndiaye were leafing through in the reserves was the handwritten list of the 147 objects that had survived the war.

The new Museum would not open its doors until 1973. The ethnographic objects, on display in four temporary exhibitions between 1949 and 1968, next became part of the permanent exhibition until 1982, then were put away in the reserves—and almost completely forgotten until the caliph's visit.

The only one who was concerned about them all those years was a former collections curator of the museum, Thierry

Vincent, now archivist at the municipal archives who, on my first visit to Fort Tourneville, told me about their five moves, the flood in 1994, and the inventories to track down.

When I had asked him what he thought about the restitutions, he had admitted to being of two minds.

"Where will those objects be displayed and in what conditions?" he had asked before he reconsidered: "At the same time, we are in no position to teach any lessons about that."

Today one of the rare visible traces of Archinard in Le Havre is his tomb. One morning, I went all the way up to the Sainte-Marie Cemetery. The pink sky became blue as I walked along the main path. The family vault was easy to find, section 51, row 6, plot 2. A bushy shrub hid part of the pillar that adorned the marble slab, eroded by moss in some places. Time and bad weather had gotten the better of a few of the letters and some of the numbers, which we now just had to guess. There were twelve names engraved on the white stone, including that of Naba Kamara, her first name almost entirely erased, as was the day of her death in January 1921. She was forty-three years old.

THE DRUM OF DOUBT

AIX-EN-PROVENCE, FRANCE
NATIONAL OVERSEAS ARCHIVES

The tone was formal and firm. It has been almost a year since fifteen boxes which had arrived from the French Sudan were still hanging around in the premises of the central colonial supply Store, including fourteen boxes from Ségou, "which together weighed 1,166 kilos [. . .] and contained various documents, tents, collectibles, flint guns, a camp bed, etc. [. . .] placed in storage at the Central Store with no known destination." It was October 30, 1891. The Store's office manager wrote to the Under-Secretariat of the Colonies. It was time to find out what to do with all that stuff.

> *"These various packages, still in storage at the Store, are quite inconvenient," the bureau chief wrote. "It is my honor to ask you Sir, Chief of the 2nd division, if you would kindly consider whether it may be possible to donate their contents somewhere (museums, an exhi-*

bition, etc.) as was discussed during the Central Store's special committee meeting."

The office that received the letter merely sent it along to another department, like a hot potato that everyone passed along. In December 1891, the bureau chief took up his pen once again to indicate that there were two additional crates of "gold materials" and asked: "which destination would be most suitable to donate them?"

It was my first day at the National Overseas Archives, more commonly referred to as ANOM, in Aix-en-Provence, in the south of France. I had come to find out more about the fate of the Treasure of Ségou, those crates I had seen in the archives in Dakar, which were about to be sent off to France, after a first sorting in Kayes by the commission that had been set up for the occasion: an artillery captain, an assistant commissioner, and a pharmacist—improvised experts in gold jewelry.

I was hoping to find the next part of the story here, in this large bright room with its rows of light wood tables, wide like the room. I requested the first box, which I went to look for in the "issuance of documents" corner, where readers waited in line for each collection on reserve. Then, like the other readers, I brought my box to the place they had assigned to me, in a silent and studious procession, filled with the hope that my digging would lead to the information I was missing, to the missing puzzle piece that would shed light on everything else.

As I opened the box, I suddenly stopped to wonder how we would do research in the future, when all the documents became digital files, PDFs, Word documents, and PowerPoints. I had developed an appreciation for old paper throughout my long investigation, for the cardboard file folders, paperback ledgers, scribbled drafts, the connections and upstrokes of letters I had to decipher on loose leaf pages or letterhead. I felt somehow closer to the past as I turned the pages.

In the box labeled SOUD 1, there were four file folders, including 2A, titled "Crates from Ségou." After I had read three of the documents, it was clear that, in Paris, no one was in any hurry to deal with the objects Archinard had sent. The crates had arrived at #4 rue Jean-Nicot in December 1890 and had been waiting there since, on that small street in the 7th arrondissement. The delivery note, written three months earlier, on September 2, 1890, presented a detailed list of the contents of the fourteen crates.

In crates 1-3 were the books and manuscripts—487 in all, including "29 Korans." The fourth crate contained "one of El Hadj Oumar's tents," the fifth "two copper canes from Madani, two parasols, eleven harnesses, three talismans, a child's toy, a pair of women's shoes, a mosquito net from Ségou, twenty-five textiles from Ségou, a registry, seven tablets with Arabic inscriptions, and a saber that belonged to El Hadj Oumar."

I mulled over the list. So, a saber really was taken from Ségou—a saber that someone, probably Archinard, had attributed to El Hadj Oumar Tall. Based on what? The inventory said nothing about it, nor did the other documents I found in the box. A telegram, sent from Kayes November 13, 1890, suggested that Archinard wanted to give his version of the story: "Two shipping notices have been sent—one to the Colonies, one to Bordeaux—for fourteen crates of Ségou objects. After receipt could be placed in storage at the Colonies Museum until my return to allow me to provide information and complete it for an interesting collection."

Was this saber the one that Archinard had seized from young Abdoulaye's hands, as the Tall family explained? The image of the boy defending his mother, weapon in hand, was evoked time and time again by everyone in Senegal, even by Professor Abdoulaye Sokhna Diop, who refuted that the saber belonged to El Hadj Oumar Tall—as if the symbolic weight of that image, of a child attacking someone much stronger than him, epitomized another version of history: the courage of resisting the colonizer even in the face of the obvious asymmetry of weapons. That image masked another image, that of men who had fled the city, leaving women and children behind.

I went back to the inventory in Kayes.

[In crate #6] there was "a trunk from Ségou containing other pages from books in Arabic, two pairs of stirrups, twenty basketry objects, a board and a copper plate with Arabic inscriptions." Three crates each containing a water jug, three other crates containing "a tabala from Ségou", "two tabalas from Ségou" and "one tabala from Ouéssébougou." (How many drums had Archinard taken?) There was also one "cot" (crate 14), "two flintlock pistols from Madani" and two flags (crate 12). As for the jewels, they were in two other crates: crate #9 A containing 48 silver pieces, crate #20 holding 48 pieces of gold jewelry, inventoried on two other lists. There were therefore 96 pieces of jewelry in total, some of which were described with precision.

That was not the case of the contents of the other fourteen crates. It was impossible to determine which were the "eleven harness objects", or what "El Hadj Oumar's saber" looked like exactly, or what distinguished the tabalas from Ségou from those from Ouéssébougou. The inventory gave no detail. I wondered whether retracing their trajectory today, to the reserves of the Quai Branly Museum, of the Natural History Museum in Le Havre or of the Army Museum, was even worth it.

When the crates arrived in Paris in December 1890, a new committee was designated to open them, sort them, and decide where to send them. The jewelry was appraised, and, in March of 1891, the committee delivered its opinion. It believed that the collection was "of significant value."

Some [of the objects], in fact, have historical significance, and almost all the others are useful ethnographic documents, at least the jewelry, whose estimated worth is generally quite high, does show some artistic value.

The committee recommended that the books and manuscripts be given to the School of Living Oriental Languages, "where they could be usefully deciphered." As for the other objects, including the jewelry, they should be sent to a museum, the committee suggested: "The Permanent Exhibition of the Colonies [...] seemed naturally suited to receive them, but in the event that the Exhibition of the Colonies could not house them due to lack of space, they should be placed on display at the Trocadéro Museum of Ethnography, which already holds collections of the same kind."

However, it would be two more years before the objects left the Central Store. A note detailed the destinations: eight crates of various objects were sent to the curator of the Permanent Exhibition of the Colonies, four packages containing the manuscripts were sent to the National Library. The Exhibition also received "four crates of gold and silver."

Lastly, three crates "containing El Hadj Oumar's saber and three tabalas from Ouéssébougou" were being stored at the Central Store to be returned to Colonel Archinard. The bureau chief, determined to finally rid himself of those very cumbersome spoils of war, proposed an alternative solution: "I am waiting for orders for their temporary storage, if necessary, at the Exhibition, as space is still lacking here and needs to be cautiously reserved for ordinary supplies in transit."

(Not everyone approved of the decision. A few days prior to the transfer, another office of the Under Secretary of the Colonies sent a letter asking what criteria established that the

Permanent Exhibition and the National Library should inherit the entirety of the loot, when they had advised allocating part of it to the Trocadéro Museum and to the School of Oriental Languages.)

That was how the jewelry ended up on display for the public for the first time at the Permanent Exhibition of the Colonies in 1893, which was reported in that very first archival document I came across at the beginning of my investigation, the article in *L'Illustration*. It was at there that journalists had doubted the African origin of some of the jewelry, deeming it too sophisticated.

Later, I was rummaging through my external hard drive, which was filling up fast. It stored my own treasure, namely the sources I had been gleaning over the past two years: archival documents, PDFs of articles, Internet links, bibliographical references, photos of the places I had been and people I had met, recorded interviews and background noise, notes I had written in trains, planes, buses, as well as in archive reading rooms in Dakar, Saint-Louis, Paris, Le Havre, and now here, in Aix-en-Provence. I was looking for that article in *L'Illustration* with the description of those objects on display. I wanted to know if the saber had remained in the crates said to be Archinard's or if it had ended up at the Permanent Exhibition. *L'Illustration* said nothing about it. I went back to the article from *Nature* magazine. Journalist Adrien Barbusse had noticed the weapon attributed to El Hadj Oumar Tall and described it like this: "The saber [...] is garlanded with leather straps, finished with tassels and holstered in a sheath, also leather, blackened by time."

I re-examined the photo of the saber exhibited in Dakar, at the Museum of Black Civilizations, the object that had been "returned" to Senegal, but which the Tall family said was not "the real one." The sheath was indeed "blackened by time," but there was no trace of the leather straps, nor of any tassels. What if the returned object was not the one that had been taken in Ségou? If that were the case, where had this saber come from, the one the guides at the museum in Dakar were showing to visitors as having belonged to El Hadj Oumar Tall, which the Tall family considered not to be El Hadj Oumar's real saber, and which Professor Abdoulaye Sokhna Diop saw above all as an object manipulated by politicians? And where was the saber that had been exhibited in 1893?

Another burning question for me was: what if Archinard had simply made up the prestigious origins of the objects of those collections? After all, wasn't it more glorious to bring back a "saber that had belonged to El Hadj Oumar" rather than just any old weapon found in a corner of the fort? I thought about how the troop commander took such pains to build up his image in Le Havre, about the narrative he created around his career, always connecting it to something bigger, to France's colonial project in Africa. I thought about the three tabalas from Ségou and Ouéssébougou, and wondered about the fate of the two others, the ones that did not end up at the

Museum in Le Havre. Had they been destroyed in the museum fire in 1944? Plus, I said to myself, increasingly overcome with doubt, what could guarantee, apart from the story Archinard himself told, that the drum with its slashed skin that I'd seen in Dakar and then in Le Havre was the one that stopped beating when the Bandiougou-Diara chief had been blown up with his family? And whether the story about the slashed skin, retold on the Museum's Internet website, were nothing but a narrative constructed in hindsight, yet another in a symbolic battle between each of its protagonists?

My questions were dizzying. I wondered what direction my investigation was going to take: would I end up at a chic dinner party at the Frascati Hotel looking out at the English Channel, or would I be having a traditional Senegalese soupou kandja, along the river?

THE INFORMANT

AIX-EN-PROVENCE, FRANCE
NATIONAL OVERSEAS ARCHIVES

The following day, I went back to the archives. During the night, I had dreamt about verifying the inventories and handwritten letters with their polite greetings as they were sent from one office to the next. I resumed my search. My mind had gone numb.

Crate #851, file #2,284. I jumped ahead by thirty years, traveling to February 1921. A new committee was to meet. The focus was still the jewelry. The reason: an anonymous letter had been received denouncing a theft alleged to have occurred ten years earlier, whereas the objects had not been exhibited for several years and were stored away in a sealed crate at the accountant's office, the minutes of the committee's first meeting specified. It was therefore necessary to check out the claim.

Reading that typed document immediately snapped me out of my torpor. What was this all about? I remembered the other two thefts, the one which had taken place at the Army Museum in 1914, and the one at the Palais de la Porte Dorée in 1937. So, there was a third? Or rather a first?

Mr. Ponel, editor at the Agency of the Colonies, recalled the collection's origin:

> *[The objects in question] are from the liquidation of the Permanent Exhibition of the Colonies after which they were divided into three distinct batches: the first comprising objects of historical interest, given by the Colonial Office to be stored at the Army Museum, [...]; the second made up of jewelry that had been melted down into gold bars to be sold [...]; and, finally, the third comprised the remaining jewelry and objects from the colonies, including coins and medals, which remained at the Palais-Royal.*

As I read on, I realized that the collection in question not only included the Treasure of Ségou, but also additional jewelry. Mr. Ponel, who had defined the scope of the file for the committee, noted that there was no inventory of any of it at the Colonial Office—a state agency that was created in 1899 and renamed the General Agency of the Colonies in 1919. The only document he had in hand was an inventory that had been sent with an anonymous letter. That was proof, the informant wrote: the objects noted in blue pencil in that inventory—which date from 1910—were exactly those that had been pilfered.

As I dug deeper into the file, I found that letter, which was addressed to "Mister Director of the Colonial Office," labeled "Personal" underlined in the upper right-hand corner. The informant not only denounced the theft of the "jewels from the Ahmadou's Treasure"—but he also accused someone in particular, one Armand Lemaire, a former accounting officer at the Office:

> *Rejecting outright the silver objects, and worried about getting caught wearing the medals inscribed with a date and the memory of events of the period, he instead went for the gold bars, the bracelets and the necklaces, which his wife must still possess, because she had adorned herself with those bracelets to go to a ball.*
>
> *Mr. Lemaire wrote in the inventory log in blue pencil, specifying the jewelry and the bars he stole, as you can see. He also took that inventory with him so nobody would notice the theft.*

The committee had to review everything more closely. They compared the informant's inventory with the list of objects the Army Museum had received, also dating from 1910, and found that the two corresponded. The next step was to proceed to physical verification of the objects. The informant seemed to be correct: indeed, one gold bar, two gold earrings, all the gold filigree bracelets, pieces of coral and silver jewelry, and a chiseled brooch with gold and silver leaves were missing. The official report indicated that a silver filigree tray and a silver ewer, which "currently adorns Mr. the Director's office" were also missing.

However, according to the committee, none of those pieces of jewelry were part of the Ségou Treasure. I was almost disappointed, caught up in my own hunt for a story. Disheartened, I continued to decipher the rest of the documents which went back through time, trying to find out where the objects had gone after the Permanent Exhibition of the Colonies, which closed in 1896.

According to an initial inventory prepared by a jeweler named A. Cartier in 1897, probably after the exhibition closed, four pieces from "the Ahmadou's Treasure" were missing: a delicate gold necklace, a leather necklace with a fine filigree clasp, a leather necklace with a gold filigree star-shaped plate, and a coral glass bead and leather necklace." From 96 pieces of jewelry, we were now down to 92.

In 1900, the jewelry was again exhibited at the Senegal Pavilion at the World's Fair, then in 1906, at the colonial exhibition in Marseille. In 1910, seven gold bracelets were sold then melted down to balance the accounts at the Colonial Office.

That same year, the 85 pieces of jewelry that remained were put in storage at the Army Museum following a standoff between the Ministry of War and the Minister of the Colonies. The Ministry of War wanted to recover the ownership of the jewelry, while the Minister of the Colonies wanted to simply put it in storage, in other words, place them on loan. Backing up the Minister of War's request was Archinard. He was the one who gave the idea to General Niox, the director of the museum, and who insisted on it to the authorities when they were awaiting a decision. I had the impression that, now that he was a general and far away from the Sudan from where he had been dismissed only a few years after the siege of Ségou, the Le Havre officer was determined to keep his African legend alive, and that the objects would play a significant role in that. The director of the Colonial Office, for his part, would have preferred that the objects be placed in a colonial museum, "not only out of curiosity, but as a specimen of Sudanese workmanship, which could very well be made by amateurs or imitators." Ironically, that did eventually happen, but not until 1933, one year after Archinard's death, when the jewelry was added to the permanent collection of the Colonies Museum in the Palais de la Porte Dorée.

Regarding the saber, box #851 gave me no new information. It only concerned the jewelry. I also did not know where the tent, the harnesses, the water jugs or the child's toy ended up. Had they been transferred with the jewelry to the Army Museum, or had they stayed at the Colonial Office? Had Archinard recuperated the saber and the drums that had been set aside for him at the Central Store, then placed on display at the Permanent Exhibition? Perhaps there were answers somewhere in the reserves of those archives, but I did not really know where to look anymore.

So, I decided to follow another lead: Abdoulaye. Officially, he was a ward of the French State; "it's the government who looks after him," Archinard reminded his audience speaking from the terrace of the Frascati Hotel in 1891. So, part of his story was here, in the boxes that could only be checked out of the reserve at specific times. I took out the list of classifications I had written down over the past two years and requested the first box, then the second, then the third. I spent two days, from morning to night, searching for any trace of the kidnapped child. I combed through letters between colonial services, invoices, notes and reports. And through those administrative documents of the French State, I was able to see the child growing up as he became an adolescent, then a young adult.

THE YOUNG PRINCE

AIX-EN-PROVENCE, FRANCE
NATIONAL OVERSEAS ARCHIVES

Mr. Under Secretary of State,

It is my honor to inform you, upon the request of Mr. Lieutenant-Colonel, Senior Commander of the French Sudan, that I have granted first-class travel aboard the Marine couriers' ocean liner, leaving Dakar on the 7th of this month, to young Abdoulaye, son of Ahmadou Cheikhou, whom, for political reasons, Mr. Archinard insisted on taking with him.

Mr. Archinard also took, at his request and with my approval, a document he wished to retain, noting commitment to the reimbursement of young Abdoulaye's travel costs, in the event that you do not give your approval for this trip.

The expense was charged to chapter 8 of the colonial service.

With profound respect, Mr. Under Secretary, your very obedient servant.

The letter was signed by Clément Thomas, then governor of Senegal. That is how Abdoulaye's journey to France began, three months before the crates of objects had left Dakar. According to Archinard, it was urgent that the boy leave. He had written the evening before to Mr. Thomas to explain.

> *You are aware, Mr. Governor, of the political interest in demanding this child's departure. There is not enough time to consult the department and provide the necessary details.*
>
> *Keeping Abdoulaye for even a few additional days in Saint-Louis runs the risk of some kind of manipulation or his kidnapping. Besides, this child has gotten used to me. He saw that I have established a good relationship with his old mother whose consent for her son's departure I insisted upon. He has been in my charge for a long time and has shown affection for me and, above all, trust. Having him travel a little later, without me, would be more difficult, and he would certainly react with fear.*

Abdoulaye and Archinard embarked for Bordeaux on August 7, 1890. Upon their arrival, Archinard bought outfits for the child, then took him to the capital, and was later reimbursed to the sum of 772 francs. He was then entrusted to the Isle de Sales family, acquaintances of Archinard who lived at 23, rue Singer, in the 16th arrondissement in Paris. The Mister was an architect and worked at 3, rue d'Alger, between the Tuileries Garden and Place Vendôme. Abdoulaye began his Parisian life in the beautiful neighborhoods of the capital. He was eleven years old.

On August 26, 1890, a tricycle supplier, whose name was indecipherable in his signature, sent a letter thanking the Under Secretary of State.

> *Thank you for choosing my company to supply the tricycle intended for young Prince Abdoulaye. The tricycle, which has been tuned up and checked with the greatest care, was delivered yesterday, and I hasten to inform you, Mr. Under Secretary of State, that I am entirely at your service to have my son, who in charge of the management of student cycling sports schools at the Pré Catelan Velodrome, provide the prince with all necessary lessons, free of charge of course.*

I imagined Abdoulaye on his tricycle, pedaling through the Bois de Boulogne. He had just arrived in France. The trees were all species unknown to him. The heat was not what he was used to, that of the rainy season, so swollen with moisture that it stuck to the skin from morning till evening, between intense bursts of storms, pouring down torrents of water then dissipating. He was introduced to Toubab clothes, which he had to wear to tolerate the new climate. And what's more, around him, there were only Toubabs, however, there, they were not all like Archinard, giving orders, defining the law, and believing they were the strongest. There were also Toubabs who were servants, who did the cleaning and served the meals. And then there was Prince Abdoulaye on his tricycle. Who was he at eleven years old as he navigated that world? What did he see in the gazes that fell upon him in the streets of Paris: admiration that one reserved for a future king who had come from elsewhere or curiosity about an exotic specimen? The same curiosity with which one saw the objects at the Trocadéro Museum or at the Permanent Exhibition of the Colonies? I wondered if the skulls that had been brought back from the colonies had been on display in the museums of the capital during that time, whether the child, Abdoulaye, knew about it and what he thought about it. In his social circles, the only person who connected with the world he had known to that point, who really knew where he came from was Archinard. Suddenly, I was remembering my first European autumn, in Finland, feeling extremely alone in a society where I had no reference points, despite my physical appearance which made me blend into the masses, unlike Abdoulaye in the Parisian streets of 1890. I was fifteen years old, felt entirely out of place, like a complete stranger, and it was unbearable.

One year after he had arrived, in 1891, Archinard wrote to the Under Secretary of State of the Colonies requesting that Abdoulaye be authorized to participate in major military operations.

Abdou Laï wishes to become one of our native officers and perhaps in the not-too-distant future you would like to send him back to Senegal to stay with his uncle, our ally, Aguibou. I believe it is of the utmost importance while he is in France to have him witness this great deployment of forces which he will certainly remember and talk about upon his return to the Sudan. Abdou Laï has just written to me asking to participate in those operations.

Aguibou, one of Ahmadou's brothers, had in fact decided to rally behind France—it was a way to guarantee his power in the conflicts that were raging between El Hadj Oumar Tall's successors. Clearly, Archinard had a plan for the allied leader's young nephew. The request was accepted and Abdoulaye, then twelve years old, observed the operations for six days, with his guardian, Mr. de l'Isle de Sales.

I wondered where Abdoulaye went to school. I knew that in 1894, when he was fifteen, he was a student at the Lycée Janson-de-Sailly, a reputable public high school in the 16th arrondissement. But there was nothing in the archives about his schooling prior to that. For years there was nothing, absolutely no trace of Abdoulaye's daily life. There was only mention of the exceptional, extraordinary moments like that authorization, which granted him travel to Senegal to see his mother again in 1893. At that time, he was fourteen.

On August 20, 1893, Abdoulaye embarked in Bordeaux.

Several documents attested to that trip: the report to the Under Secretary of State for the Colonies on the planned departure "in accordance with the promise made by Mr. Colonel Archinard to young Abdoulaye, son of Ahmadou", the telegram requesting "3rd class liner. August 20th, Destination Dakar," the notice of departure from Bordeaux, the proposal, approved by the administration, to pay 500 francs to Mr. de l'Isle de Sales for "meager travel expenses and the purchase of gifts."

To justify those costs, Mr. de l'Isle de Sales drew up a detailed list, on letterhead from his architectural firm, with the title "Objects Abdoulaye would like to bring to the Sudan." The list included letter paper, envelopes, twelve postage stamps, notebooks, quill pens, quill stands, a pencil, a ruler and an ink well, candles, candlesticks, lanterns and matches, scissors, paper cutters, razors and lighters, binoculars, a thermometer, a barometer and a compass, pillows and blankets, a wallet, a pocket sundial, an asbestos filter, a box of paints, a bellows, an alarm clock, a jute armchair and a matching chair, a revolver for his uncle Aguibou, maps of France, a map of Paris and picture books for his niece, cotton fabrics for his mother and sister, and pocket money in the amount of 140 francs.

The fourteen-year-old adolescent returned as a prodigal son, his arms full of gifts. He too brought his treasure. A few weeks prior to his departure, a telegram was sent to the Kayes post office: "Send cable when mother of young Abdoulaye has arrived in Kayes or is on her way as agreed." In the same register other dispatches were compiled concerning the war

Archinard was waging against Ahmadou. Since its siege of Ségou, the French had gained ground, profiting from internal dissent in the kingdom to forge alliances. On April 29, 1893, Ahmadou's last bastion, Bandiagara, was taken. Archinard entered the city with Aguibou, Abdoulaye's uncle, who became the leader of the kingdom of Macina, signaling the fall of the Toucouleur Empire.

Archinard had thus waited to definitively vanquish the father before authorizing his son's return, four months later. There was no gift for his father on Abdoulaye's list, only the revolver for his uncle, an ally of the French. Whose idea was that? A fourteen-year-old kid's or Archinard's?

I could not find any documents relating to the trip. I did not know whether Abdoulaye saw his uncle Aguibou to hand him his revolver, whether he had read the picture book to his niece, or whether his mother and sister liked the fabrics. Nor did I know whether he talked about his stay in the letters he sent from Saint-Louis or Kayes to his friends—how does one talk about coming home when it is no longer really home?—or whether he had drawn those rediscovered landscapes, whether he still remembered his mother tongue, which he had probably not spoken for three years. I imagined him confronting his childhood memories, with a perspective that had changed since he had grown up, with eyes that had seen another horizon—lower and grayer—and skin that had learned to withstand the cold. I did not know when he returned to Paris, whether he had cried when he left or whether, on the contrary, he had been relieved to return to a world that had become his own, or both at the same time, that bittersweet feeling experienced by those who navigate between two worlds, two languages, two senses of belonging. All that I knew was, on February 11, 1894, he wrote a letter to Archinard:

My Dear Colonel,

I confirm my letter, written the 5th, which crossed with yours.

You told me that you may be back around the 9th. So, I waited until then to tell you that you can come any day for lunch or dinner. Inform me the day before with a note.

I hope that this time nothing will deprive me of that pleasure.

I am very sad to see the disaster that has just occurred at the Bonnier column; remember I recently told you that the Sudan would suffer from your absence. The current events confirm this.

Mr. and Mrs. de l'Isle de Sales send you their best regards and I send you my most heartfelt affection.

Yours,

Abdou Lahi ben Ahmadou

Abdoulaye would soon be fifteen. He was writing with adult expressions and signing his name using the Latin alphabet as well as the Arabic alphabet. Archinard was no longer in Africa. He had been dismissed as troop commander. The letter was part of one of Archinard's private correspondence files, kept separately in the archives as they were too fragile to be handled like the other boxes. I had to request special permission to access it, indicating the document I was interested in, and ask for a photograph of it. It arrived with a small handwritten label, next to the letter, which read: "Letter from young Abdou-Lahi, son of Sultan Ahmadou defeated by Archinard. After the fall of Ségou in 1890, the sultan's family fell into Archinard's hands, who brought their son, Abdou-Lahi, to France. He was sent to Lycée Janson-de-Sailly, entered Saint-Cyr and died shortly thereafter. He had a faithful attachment to Colonel Archinard."

I wondered who had written that label. Was it Archinard, sorting his mail before he died? Or his wife or his nephew who oversaw his estate?

Later, I would contact Lycée Janson-de-Sailly, asking if they had any information about the young man's schooling. A volunteer at the alumni association responded dubiously to me initially: "It is a sensitive topic." Afterward I received a summary of his grades and assessments. Those were the only documents that remained of his adolescent life. That was how I learned that in September of 1894 he entered the "modern" course track, meaning without any Latin or Greek; that at fifteen he was already older than his classmates; that he had excellent marks that year, which explains that the following year he would move directly up to a "science" course track. The archives in Aix-en-Provence did not mention that period of his life. On the other hand, in July 1896, when Abdoulaye was finishing his last year of high school (a more challenging year though he was completing "regular work" and with "very good behavior"), there was an unsigned note addressed to the military technical committee of the Under Secretary of the Colonies. It was accompanied by "a letter with which the lieutenant-governor of the French Sudan was requesting that young Abdou Lahi, Ahmadou's son, be sent back to the colony at the end of the current school year." What had happened for such a demand to be made? The letter to which the note referred was not in the file. Impossible to know any more about it. The note ended with a request:

The Secretary General would be grateful to General Archinard if, after he has become aware of this letter and the reservations it has provoked on the part of the Governor General of French West Africa, he would be kind enough to let him know his opinion on the evaluation of the measure requested by Lieutenant Colonel Trentinian.

Archinard's reply was not in the file either. It was as if that note had been lost. It had no concrete follow-up, since the following file concerned Abdoulaye's request to go to Saint-Cyr.

On August 17, 1898, Mr. de l'Isle de Sales and Abdoulaye

wrote to the Minister of Colonies, requesting the young man's admission, as a native, now nineteen years old, to the Saint-Cyr Military Academy.

"Having had the young Abdou Lahi at my home for eight years," Mr. de l'Isle de Sales wrote, "I can attest to his feelings of loyalty and affection towards France."

The young man also wrote a long letter explaining his motivations.

Mr. Minister,

Eager to show my gratitude to France for the hospitality and education she has given me, I would also like to show her my complete and absolute dedication by serving in her glorious army.

In 1897, I had the honor of being admitted to the Saint-Cyr examinations. This year, following circumstances that were out of my control, I was obligated to interrupt my studies and therefore failed my examinations.

I have one remaining hope, and I leave it to your great benevolence. Please allow me to continue the courses at the Saint-Cyr Military Academy of Saint-Cyr as a native.

Mr. Deputy Director of the Infantry at the Ministry of War was kind enough to give his assurances to Mr. de l'Isle de Sales that this favor, which the French government entrusted to me, would be immediately granted to me with a favorable word from the Minister of Colonies.

I therefore dare hope, Mr. Minister, that you will grant me this protection and patronage, which were promised to me upon my arrival in France, and I will do my best to show that I am worthy through my eagerness to serve loyally and patriotically.

What were those "circumstances" that prevented Abdoulaye from preparing his exams as he would have liked? Nobody said anything about it, but for them to be mentioned like that, I thought to myself, the minister must have known.

Barely a month later, on September 10, 1898, Abdoulaye picked up his pen again to write once more to the minister.

Mr. Minister,

The Director of Africa was kind enough, through Mr. Henri des Houx, to share your words of kindness towards me and the conditions on which you place your high and paternal protection.

I subscribe willingly to all those conditions. If you would allow me to continue as a native the courses at the Academy of Saint-Cyr, I hope to have nothing to fear from the supervision of my leaders, and to manage through my conduct to delete the unfavorable grades contained in my file.

I have the firm intention of becoming a loyal officer of the French army and to pay off my debt through the service and gratitude which I have established toward my new homeland in which I aim to become naturalized as soon as possible.

Furthermore, if my grades at Saint-Cyr allow me the honor of becoming an officer in two years, I agree to undertake my internship either in the Foreign Legion, as Mr. Binger has proposed, or if your Excellency wishes to take my preferences into account, with the Spahis, which are to the cavalry roughly what the Foreign Legion is to the infantry.

There, too, I will work to show that I am worthy of the esteem and trust of my leaders. After this time of trial, I ask you if I may, as of now, return to France to serve there as a French citizen in a regiment of the homeland, where I intend to stay from then on.

The same day, Henri des Houx, political editor at the newspaper Le Matin, also wrote a letter in support of Abdoulaye's request:

I can guarantee you that, having known Abdou Lahi since the first days of his stay in France, having followed closely the progress of his mind and observed his perfect loyalty, he will honor the solemn commitments that he is making at this time before you. I vouch for his loyalty, and for his keen desire to be a good servant of his adopted homeland.

He ended with: "I beg you, therefore, once again, to forget a moment of misguidedness caused by temptations too great for a child, of which he showed to me his regret, which I know to be sincere."

So, what happened in Abdoulaye's life during those two years? What "misguidedness" had he been guilty of that it caused him to be reprimanded by authorities as high up as the Ministry? I thought about the adolescent who had grown up in a foreign land that had become his own, but where he remained a native who had to submit to the humiliating exercise of expressing his gratitude to and imploring the State, embodied by the minister, in order to realize his dreams—dreams that had been instilled in him by the same person who had taken him away from his family. The authority that was deciding his future was not a relative. Nor was it the one hosting him in his home, much less Archinard who, after having imagined his predestined future, now seemed to be conspicuously silent. No, the one deciding was the French State and the minister and nothing more.

Later, when I finally laid eyes on Abdoulaye's school results, I saw that after his final year of high school he joined a preparatory class for Saint-Cyr which he repeated, two years which seemed to be difficult for the student whose assessments wavered between "average", "fair", "inconsistent" and "weak", although some professors did recognize his willingness and diligence. His history/geography and French teacher even noted: "intelligent, a good student, deserves to succeed." But it was as if something had spiraled. I reread Abdoulaye's letter to the minister, the way he described his attachment to France, his desire to be naturalized quickly and serve in the French military, in France. He was French and he claimed it. Had he known about the request made by the governor of the Sudan two years before they had sent him back to Africa?

On October 13th, the War Ministry informed the Minister of Colonies that Abdoulaye was accepted at Saint-Cyr, as a foreigner, subject to an aptitude test, and that he could then be promoted to second lieutenant, as a foreigner, in a foreign regiment. That was fine for the school that the young man was aiming for, okay for the dream nourished by Archinard for all those years, but for the French State, Abdoulaye would not be French. He would remain a native.

Things went downhill quickly. Abdoulaye did pass the aptitude exam at the end of October and got into the school, but his health deteriorated. He had barely begun classes when the Ministry of Colonies requested that the young man be examined by a doctor to say "whether, given his health status, the young native should be sent to Senegal, unless it were necessary to send him to one of the hospitals in the colony."

I had the impression that someone in the Ministry clearly wanted to get rid of Ahmadou's son, and as swiftly as possible, as if they absolutely did not want him to fit in at Saint-Cyr. Was he still being reproached for his "misguidedness?"

The doctor's report arrived in December, with a note in

blue pencil: "Very urgent." Abdoulaye was ill with tuberculosis. His right lung had advanced lesions, and the left showed signs of congestion as well. The doctor recommended a stay in a Mediterranean resort, but only "if his condition stabilized enough to allow him to make the journey safely."

As for the question the administration had posed regarding eventually sending him "back home," the doctor's verdict was definitive:

I do not think, given the severity of the rapid evolution of his ailment, that there is reason to propose that the young man be sent back to his home country, unless in the event that his illness is uncurable and thus adds a moral factor that would motivate such a determination.

Abdoulaye died three months later, on March 19, 1899, at the home of Mr. and Mrs. de l'Isle de Sales. He was only twenty years old. I found the death announcement among the letters between various offices of the Ministry of Colonies, which included one in which Mr. de l'Isle de Sales requested to reinstate the monthly payment of three hundred francs, the pension that was paid to him for being the young man's caretaker, which was interrupted when he entered Saint-Cyr. Amidst all the loquaciousness in those letters with their formalities and complicated turns of phrase, the small death announcement was outlined in black like an invitation to reverence.

Mr. and Mrs. de l'Isle de Sales, offering their respectful greetings to Mr. Guillain, Minister of the Colonies, regret to inform him of the cruel loss they have experienced on this day of their adopted son, a ward of the French government, Abdou Lahi, son of Ahmadou, the former sultan of the French Sudan, grandson of El Hadj Oumar, and student at the prestigious Saint-Cyr Military Academy.

A bill for funeral services, 570.25 francs, an oak casket, a hearse pulled by white horses, a florist's receipt, 60 francs per bouquet for fresh flowers. A telegram to the governor of Saint-Louis: "Abdou-Lahi, son of Ahmadou, deceased yesterday. Notify his mother with care."

Then, a report written by Mr. Binger, director of African Affairs, addressed to the Minister of Colonies. It was dated March 17, 1899, two days prior to Abdoulaye's death.

By letter dated January 28 of this year, Mr. Lieutenant-Governor of the Sudan, reminding the department of a communication of his predecessor, dated October 7, 1897, where the negative disposition manifested by Ahmadou's son was indicated during the trip he was making to the Sudan that year, had expressed the desire to have the native, currently a student at the prestigious Saint-Cyr Military Academy, no longer receive the credit which had been allocated to him by the colony's local budget to provide for his living expenses in France.

Having completed the studies for which Abdoulaye had been sent to France, Ahmadou's son had been authorized to take courses at our prestigious military academy, with a scholarship from the State, and, since last October, a sum of 50 francs per month had been allocated to him for his personal expenses out of the local budget account of the Sudan. But, having fallen ill, that native only made one short appearance at the prestigious Saint-Cyr Military Academy and, since then had to return to Mr. de Sales's who is demanding he be restored his pension of 300 francs for boarding him, which was being furnished to him prior to his admittance to Saint-Cyr. This state of affairs threatening to continue, it is my honor to request that the minister decide that a doctor from the colony health corps be designated for the purpose of examining the health status of Abdoulaye who, if his improvement does not seem imminent, shall be sent to a military hospital in the south of France or else out to one of our African colonies to take a position in native affairs.

So, Abdoulaye had returned to Africa a second time, in 1897, at the age of eighteen, four years after his first trip. Something had gone wrong however during that stay, something that the colonial administration had not forgiven him for, even two years afterwards, when he became ill. Paying even one cent to this native who, one way or another, had failed to fulfill his duties or his position, was out of the question. Having him join the French army was also out of the question. The rejection was violent and manifold. It was the rejection of a child who had then become an adolescent, who was then crossing the threshold into adulthood, claiming his place in a French society that he had been brought to by force.

The next section of the file was merely a succession of requests for money: money that Mr. de Sales was requesting to cover Abdoulaye's medical costs, in addition to the unpaid pension, which the administration was reluctant to pay him; the money that the colonial administration in Saint-Louis no longer wanted to see charged to its local budget for the educational fees of sons of chiefs in France: "Experience has, unfortunately, shown that [that kind of] instruction [...], by removing them from their milieu, often resulted in making them withdrawn and disgruntled." Simply sending them to France would suffice, the letter went on. We will show the young people "our factories, our monuments, our botanical gardens, etc." to "confirm the lofty ideas they already have about our power and our civilization." That way, once they are back home, "instead of being troublesome components, [they] will become valuable auxiliaries of our influence."

The minister's approval marked the end of the experiment Archinard had attempted: turning a chief's son into a loyal servant of the colony by making him French. Something had gone wrong. The child did not only see the military operations; he became witness to something else as well. Then, the child became an adolescent, and his outlook had changed in perspective as well as in depth. He had grown roots, and an assertiveness, a desire to spread his wings and to exist as a full human being. Something had gone wrong because witnessing is a dangerous and subversive act. Domination requires controlling the other's gaze and limiting its scope, whether it involves objects from elsewhere placed in museums to tell a story of natural superiority or a member of their youth who has been educated to a certain point, but who is only allowed to see what is admirable. Domination needs this double control. One does not exist without the other. Both the dominant and the dominated need to see each other as such until that gaze becomes so natural and integrated that we no longer notice it, and then even when everything around the visible shackles of domination shatters, the gaze remains, because it is part of us now. The other remains locked up inside, in an identity that has been assigned: the Black man is like this; the Toubab is like that. What had happened during that second trip to Senegal? There was perhaps one last place I could find the answers to my questions.

THE LITTLE MUTE GIRL

FRÉJUS, FRANCE
CENTER FOR THE HISTORICAL STUDY OF OVERSEAS TROOPS

In Fréjus, the mimosas were blooming. Thousands of little yellow springtime flecks amidst the umbrella pines and palm trees that came to brighten up the arid Mediterranean landscape. I walked along the road that led to the Center for the Historical Study of Overseas Troops, or CHETOM, as the regulars call it. The road, with no sidewalk or crosswalk, was not suitable for pedestrians. The Center was outside the city, on the other side of the highway between the Marine Corps Museum and a military training area. Around the building were excavators and trucks full of rubble. One of the doors had been replaced by a wooden panel, with a piece of paper on it that said: "OUT OF SERVICE." In the entrance hall, I saw some display cases filled with objects, others empty, mannequins packaged in bubble wrap, maps hanging on the walls, hidden by a jumble of objects piled up on the floor. I moved closer and saw a "Map of the Races of West Africa Supplying Senegalese Riflemen," interspersed with photos of men's profiles to illustrate each "race." I felt like I had traveled a hundred years back in time. There was no one in the hall. While I was looking for the entrance to the reading room, I jumped when I saw a mannequin wearing a uniform, a red kepi and a navy frock coat. He had a beer in his hand and was staring at me from the coat check.

"Welcome! You're in luck. We're going to be closing in a few days. The museum has been under construction for almost two years now. Up to now, the archives have remained open, but we will have to close them for the final months. We expect to reopen next September," the archivist explained, as he led me down to a small reading room with three tables in the building's basement.

Now all those piles on the ground floor, the excavators and the USE OTHER DOOR sign made sense.

"I got you the boxes you asked for. Which one would you like to start with?"

To be honest, I had no idea. The archivist had provided me with descriptions of their contents, but none of them mentioned Abdoulaye, so I chose one randomly. I had to start somewhere. After two years in the archives, I had learned that the information I was looking for could be hidden anywhere, and it could also not exist at all. This time, I was hoping to find it in Archinard's personal papers.

The first box contained six differently colored cardboard folders, which I leafed through one by one. Orange folder: individual mobilization order of April 16, 1914, individual registration, letters received from the Ministry of War. Red folder: Archinard's medals and nominations to military posts, Legion of honor, letters from Saigon for the Medal of Order for the King of Cambodia. Mauve folder: letters from Archinard to Borgnis-Desbordes, Gallieni, and other colonial officers. Pink folder: various awards, annual account balances. When I got to the green folder, which opened with a "handwritten report by General Archinard on the overhaul of the squadron of Sudanese Spahis," I started to despair. Next was the letter from the cabinet of the Grand Chancellor of the Legion of Honor, written in April 1890, congratulating Archinard for the siege of Ségou and suggesting that he come and relax in the countryside. Then a speech given at an awards ceremony at the Legion of Honor's school for young girls in July of 1923, which I read hastily, almost for a little peace of mind; two years'-worth of archives had also made me understand that if you're looking for something, you must leave no stone unturned, and you had to decipher every page.

And then, I found Naba Kamara.

It once happened—Archinard was telling the students to whom he had promised to discuss the condition of young black girls—*that I brought back to France a little black girl, about six or seven years old, and I'm going to tell you this so you can see just how quickly these little savages become attuned to the most civi-*

lized people, and how unfair it would be to believe that they are inferior in heart and mind.

He went on:

One day, after the assault and capture of a large village along the banks of the Niger, which only got rich by trading in slaves, I saw some abandoned children in a troop encampment. They were to be distributed among the freed villages, the Catholic and Protestant missions, or else sent to Saint-Louis to be handed over to the local chief of Justice, their legal guardian.

While I was inquiring about it, a nice little girl, black as coal, ran to my side and threw herself against me, her little arms hugging my leg, and wouldn't let go. Was she to be beaten? Was she seeking my protection? I did not know, but humbled by her gesture, I reassured her and entrusted her to one of our black interpreters so that he could keep her with his family.

And so, in Archinard's narrative, Naba was the one who chose him. I did not know whether or not to believe it. From Aix-en-Provence, the drum of doubt was banging in my head the moment Archinard spoke. He went on:

At the end of the campaign, I asked the local chief of Justice to issue her a certificate of freedom and to place her in my care, thinking that she would be welcome in the family of one of my sisters with the company of her three little daughters. She was indeed joyously received, my nieces considered her a sister, their mother had her educated with them, and she responded to the affection shown to her with an unfailing loyalty and devotion.

What had little Naba thought when she arrived in France, in 1889, one year before Abdoulaye? And what was going on in Archinard's mind when he asked his sister to look after an African girl? Was it his way of adopting a child, of maintaining a connection with Africa even in Le Havre? He was an officer who remained single until he was fifty years old, but who was known in Africa to have had four "little wives," all local African women in the colony. Obviously, he said nothing about any of that as he spoke to those young girls at the Legion of Honor. Instead, he told the rest of the story about Naba:

When, however, between two campaigns, I was coming back to France and going to Le Havre, my sister told me of her astonishment at seeing Naba change her demeanor each time I was there. I thought of the time she had seen me for the first time, the battle, the sounds of gunfire and cannons firing, the disorderly flight of an entire large village, which may have struck her imagination in a painful and resounding way. But later, when she had become a little young woman, fully French, full of distinction, surrounded by everyone's esteem, she herself said when she saw me that she always wondered whether I would take her back to Sudan. Her new family meant a lot to her. She died two years ago from an infectious flu, at a little over forty years old, and she was accompanied to the family vault by a rather large crowd who wanted to show their sympathy.

Later, as I was rummaging through another box, I found Naba again, in letters Archinard had written to Mademba Sy, an African member of his staff, whom he would later crown fama (king) of Sansanding, and to whom he would give two of Ahmadou Tall's daughters as wives. In those letters he wrote from France in 1889 and 1890, Archinard gave news of the little girl:

My little Naba is very happy in my family where she is having fun with my nieces," he wrote on August 27, 1889. "When they play in their little toy car, she is always the one riding while the others pull her, and Naba roars with laughter and claps her hands. They love each other very much and kiss one another like nibbling on a morsel of good bread. My sister is like me. She also likes the Negroes, it seems. She took a liking to Naba, who she dresses in European style like a little princess, and didn't want to leave her with the servants in the kitchen. She eats at the table with the family. She is smart as a whip, and she is getting along fine. Wherever she goes, she is very successful. She is well liked and receives lots of gifts—dolls, toys . . . she could open a store in no time.

One month later, as he was preparing his return to Africa, Archinard spoke again to Mademba about the little girl:

I found Naba to be superb here, and I asked her if she wanted to return to Senegal with me, but that is not how she sees it. She believes that she is white, and that her name is Naba Denny and says she still wants to stay with my family. She is very gay, very intelligent and very obliging. You will be amazed by her when you come to France.

I thought about that little girl who lived through the same experience as Abdoulaye, one year later: being uprooted, the different colors of the sky, the sun that would at times remain hidden the entire day behind clouds so dense that they would cover the horizon. What kind of adolescent, what kind of adult had she become? I wondered when it was that she had forgotten her mother tongue, or whether she still retained some words and phrases. What had she thought when she met Abdoulaye for the first time? Had she seen him as a rival or a brother? Not once did the documents I was going through allow Naba to speak. To me, she remained a mute child. I could neither see her face, "black as coal," nor hear her roaring laughter. I just could not believe that she was as happy as Archinard had so enthusiastically described her, and I would have preferred to imagine her life based on her own words, even if they had been few and far between. The only traces I had found of her were the family tomb in Le Havre and Archinard's words which spoke only to his devotion to the little girl, then of her death, and nothing in between.

After my lunch break, one last red folder awaited me. In it I found thank you letters from the mayor of Le Havre for the donations to the Natural History Museum in 1889 and 1891, those same letters of which I had already seen copies in the municipal archives. But there were also traces of older donations, given ten years earlier to the Ethnographic Museum of the Trocadéro which had just opened its doors.

Apparently, it was not enough for Archinard to bestow spontaneous gifts to the Natural History Museum in Le Havre. He was also busy responding to requests from French museums who were writing to him as well as to other military personnel to enrich their collections. In September of 1882, two years after the colonel had arrived in Senegal, Landrin, then curator of the Ethnographic Museum of the Trocadéro, wrote thanking him for his "beautiful gift." "The specimens and samples relating to the iron industry are of the utmost interest to us," he had written. The curator hoped that their collaboration would continue, and he was sending the officer some labels to nail onto the shipping crates. That way, the price of transporting them to France would be paid for by the minister, "and those labels will allow them to bypass customs, which is so dangerous for the collections."

Archinard had evidently taken his suggestion to send new shipments to heart because one year later, in 1883, the curator wrote a second letter thanking him for "the very beautiful, exquisite ethnographic collection that you sent to the museum while I was away." He suggested that they meet to catalogue the objects. Dr. Hamy, the director of the museum, further suggested that he write something about the objects he had brought back—about the morals, customs, industries, etc. of the Negroes with whom you lived there," and publish the article in his ethnography journal.

Once again, Archinard complied, and the director thanked him for it, specifying that the text would appear in the November issue. "My collection is, moreover, entirely available to you," he wrote. "It will be my pleasure to include in it whatever you agree to send me about the ethnography of the Negroes of the Upper River."

He went on expressing his regret at his lack of knowledge about the specific area:

> *Much work remains to be done on those populations at every level. Their anthropology is still in its infancy. The Paris Museum (Jardin des Plantes) has neither a skeleton nor a skull of the Toucouleur, and the Mandingos (Malinkés, Soninkés) are only represented by*

one piece. The Bambara too. Nothing from Bamouk, and nothing from the Niger Valley! And apart from the objects from Soleillet [. . .] and your small collection, we have nothing or almost nothing at the Ethnographic Museum either.

I suddenly felt anger rising inside, a wave that had surged out of nowhere, an accumulation of the violence, contempt and ignorance that the niceties of those letters obscured. Had they ever thought that behind that skull was a human being? Did they wonder how those "museum objects" had been seized?

The letter went on: "Consequently, you can provide a real service to those two establishments with whom I take the liberty of demanding your most active support. Look for one of my friends, Dr. Sabatier, the head doctor in Saint-Louis, who will be unsparing in his help to you. Tell him that I sent you."

That made me more furious. What was his role in the story, this head doctor Sabatier? Was he preparing the "objects" for shipping, in crates with the museum labels to avoid customs?

I looked up from the letter and focused on my surroundings to try to release my anger. I was in a reading room in the basement of the Center for the Historical Study of Overseas Troops. Outside spring was blooming and there I was sitting amongst the reserves waiting for the archivist to bring me the next box, surrounded by that part of history that Africa and Europe had in common, a macabre history where someone could cut off another's head and send it to a museum, thousands of miles away, ship it by boat and send it all the way to the office of a museum curator who would then register it in his inventory and then determine where it would be placed on display.

Moreover, Archinard did exactly as he was asked, in the name of science, in the interest of completing the collections. In June of 1884, the director of the Museum of Natural History wrote thanking him "for his donation [...] of two skulls from the Upper Niger."

I went from one letter to another haunted by the idea of seeing other human remains looming about amongst dancers' costumes, harnesses and musical instruments. But Archinard seemed to have focused more on the objects. No more skulls.

That was when Abdoulaye turned up in the small room. He emerged in a brown faux leather folder, filled with smaller pocket-envelopes, themselves filled with brown envelopes on which one archivist had written its contents in black marker: "Abdou Lahi ben Ahmadou's correspondence with Archinard."

I placed the pile of papers on the table, and I counted: there were ten letters in all. I arranged them in chronological order, photographed them, then gave the floor to the young adolescent. It was August 18, 1893. Abdoulaye was fourteen years old.

"YOUR GRATEFUL AND DEVOTED ABDOU LAHI BEN AHMADOU"

FRÉJUS, FRANCE, CENTER FOR THE HISTORICAL STUDY OF OVERSEAS TROOPS

Paris, August 18, 1893

My Dear Colonel,

You must have seen from the dispatch I recently sent you, which came to me from the ministry, that I no longer intended to leave.

I have lost nothing by waiting.

Yesterday, I went to see Commander Andry, who was very kind and told me that I was to leave tomorrow evening, Saturday, for Kayes, with Captain Regard, whom I already know, it seems.

My dear colonel, I thank you from the bottom of my heart for all that you have done for me until now. Thanks to you, I am going to see my mother again, and I do not have the words to express my profound gratitude.

Know that whether near or far, I will never forget you and that your memory is and will always be with me. I cannot describe my joy to you. I no longer sleep, no longer eat, and I no longer know what to do with myself anymore. I cannot believe how happy I am.

There is only one thing that pains me, and that is leaving without having seen you for so long; but I do hope to see you upon my return. I would also like to have news of your health, which I hope has improved.

Mr. and Mrs. de l'Isle de Sales also intend to have the pleasure of seeing you as soon as you arrive in Paris. In the meantime, they send you their best regards.

With all my affection from the bottom of my joyful heart.

All my best wishes to your dear family.

Your Abdou Lahi Ben Ahmadou.

Two days later, Abdoulaye embarked for Bordeaux. No trace of what he experienced during that journey.

The following letter was dated February 5, 1894, six months later.

My Dear Colonel,

It has been almost two years since I have seen you; I am starting to think that you do not like me anymore and that you no longer care to see me. As I passed by rue Saint-Lazare on Thursday, I stopped, in hopes that

I would find you there, but I was told that you were in Bordeaux. I had the pleasure of attending the St. Charlemagne banquet; students had to be at the top of their class once and in second place twice in order to attend. These are my most recent rankings this trimester: first in geometry and arithmetic, first in history and geography, first in recitation, fifth in morale, fourth in graphic drawing, thirteenth in ornamental drawing, thirteenth in calligraphy, and sixteenth in French, out of forty-one students.

I saw in those words a fifteen-year-old teenager who yearned for someone to take interest in him, who was seeking attention, after a trip to see his mother whom he had left yet another time and probably did not know when he would see her again. That year his teachers' evaluations were full of praise: "very good," "excellent," "very hard-working," "attentive," "exemplary work and behavior." Did he ever end up getting from Archinard what that letter seemed to be asking for so loudly: words of congratulations—"I am proud of you"—a few words of recognition for the child's efforts from the one who was responsible for his destiny but was no longer around?

Two years went by and no trace of the boy. Then, on June 8, 1896, Abdoulaye finished his last year of school. He was seventeen.

My Dear General,

Thank you very much again for taking such good care of me, and please forgive me once more for bothering troubling you.

It was very good to receive your letter, but, despite everything, my fears are only too well-founded. How do you expect me to be confident about this journey when my sister is with a husband whom she has married against her will? And, although Aguibou is no longer in Dinguiraye, he is in control there as I believe one of his sons is governing the country. And, my word, the son must not be any better than his father.

Thanks a million again, my dear General, for all your kindness toward me: regarding personal matters, my only concern is that I would be very grateful to have precise news of my family.

Mr. and Mrs. de Sales send you their kind regards and I my devoted affection.

Yours,

Abdou Lahi ben Ahmadou

The small note card was filled with words on both sides. I was surprised to see that Abdoulaye was so well-informed about what was happening in the French Sudan. I thought first of Archinard, at the time working at the Ministry of Colonies in Paris, then I remembered a letter I had come across in Aix-en-Provence. It was an authorization that Mr. de Sales was requesting, shortly after Abdoulaye's death, to recover a registered letter addressed to the young man from his mother, "to spare her the pain it would cause her to have the correspondence mentioning his 'death' returned." Perhaps he had also been receiving news that way. I reread the sentences about Aguibou, about Abdoulaye's sister, and "the son who must not be any better than his father." Was he thinking of his own fate when he wrote that sentence, or was he writing with the short-sightedness of an adolescent, so quick to judge that he did not always think about the weight of his words and the way they could bounce back at us like a boomerang? The juxtaposition of his worry for his sister and his mention of Aguibou made me think that the revolver he had offered to his uncle on the previous trip, three years earlier, had not been enough to establish trust. Archinard's plan to make Abdoulaye a French officer so he could be sent to serve with his uncle, which he had outlined at the time of the child's arrival in France, seemed ill-fated. I thought again about the note I had seen in the archives in Aix-en-Provence, written in July 1896, only a few weeks after that letter, asking Archinard his opinion about sending Abdoulaye back to Senegal. Had the adolescent somehow gotten wind of this request, and did he hear that he would be prevented from returning to France if he had to travel again to his home country?

One year later, on August 26, 1897, as Archinard was preparing to leave to spend two years in Cochinchina, Abdoulaye tried to see him to say good-bye in person. But it was in vain. Archinard was not in Paris and the young man had to pick up his pen once again to write to the general.

May my most heartfelt wishes protect you from the wickedness of men as you traverse the seas; and may God give you health and keep you among your friends. My sincere thanks for your advice: I will try to follow it. I understand that we cannot have friends everywhere. That is one of the laws here on earth. Besides, if it were otherwise, how could we appreciate the value of a good and honest friendship?

I saw Mr. Binger the day before yesterday and, like you, he understood the meager material demands that travel entails. Now everything is settled, though we did have some difficulty.

I believe Mr. Binger did not send the telegram he had promised me: so please kindly remind him in case he has forgotten, so that my mother can have my sister come to be with her.

Now regarding Saint-Cyr, I hope to be among those selected, but if I do not have the pleasure of being included, do not worry: I will not be discouraged, and I will continue to work to bring honor to those who have taught me to love my adopted homeland.

I wish you safe travels, my dear General, and send you my deepest affection. I hope to see you in good health again upon your return to Paris.

Your grateful and devoted
Abdou Lahi ben Ahmadou

The young man was still signing with two alphabets: in Latin letters and in Arabic script. At that time, he had been living in France for seven years but had not forgotten where he came from. Every time I saw his signature, I was reminded of his direct line of descent, which seemed to connect him to his childhood, as did the news he was evidently receiving regularly in Paris from his family to be able to support requests regarding his sister. I wondered how he was receiving them, since Archinard was getting ready to take on other duties on the other side of the world. He would no longer be there to support his young protégé's solicitations.

And in fact, things did go wrong, very wrong. The letter that followed, written barely three months later, had nothing to do with the previous ones. It was eleven pages long, written on both sides of A4 paper—pages and pages brimming with cold anger.

THE SON OF THE VANQUISHED SULTAN AHMADOU

FRÉJUS, FRANCE
CENTER FOR THE HISTORICAL STUDY OF OVERSEAS TROOPS

Paris, November 11, 1897
My Dear General,

I have been back in France since October 29th.

I was not accepted at Saint-Cyr and before I decide if I should continue to prepare myself for this school, despite all the rudeness and humiliation I was subjected to by the representatives of France in Senegal and in the Sudan, I want to have a brief exchange about it with you.

Certainly Mr. de l'Isle de Sales must have told you, according to the letter I wrote to him from Saint-Louis, that my intention was to wait to send word to you until I was in Kayes and could see my entire family. But, unfortunately, you yourself know that unforeseen events are common and that most often we become frustrated by our most intimate desires. Now to bore you a bit, I am going to ask your permission to tell you about the misery I was subjected to in Senegal and in the Sudan.

Therefore, I will go back to September 4, 1897, the day I arrived in Dakar.

Following the instructions that had been given to me as a so-called itinerary that I had received from the Ministry prior to my departure, I went to the delegate of the interior to obtain a requisition or payment for my mileage allowance. But since that honorable civil servant had not received anything, not a single order concerning me, neither from Paris nor from Saint-Louis, I was obliged to embark at my own expense.

Believe me, my dear General, had that been all, I would have let it go without uttering a word, but that was only the beginning of the rigamarole they wanted me to go through to the benefit of those who have the ardent desire of proving their zealousness, and doing so in the most appalling ways.

There I was in Saint-Louis on the evening of the 5th. The next morning at 9 o'clock, I ran to the residence. I introduced myself to Mr. Delvaux, Mr. Chaudié's Chief of Staff. He received me in that cordial manner that is so characteristic of the way Black people are treated in Senegal and dependencies: I stood there in front of *him for forty-five minutes, and he did not even deign to offer me a seat.*

He informed me that they did not know where my mother was: he had sent a cable to Matam to which they had replied that my mother had left several days before. Two more telegrams were sent to Kayes. Needless to say, they went unanswered. So, I asked Mr. Delvaux if I had to continue my trip despite the near certainty that I would not find a single member of my family: in my opinion, it was better to return to France. In an authoritative tone, Mr. Delvaux replied that it did not matter, that I had permission to go and spend a few days in Kayes, and that I must go there anyway.

I yielded to that decision and ask to present my respects to Mr. Ballay, interim governor of Senegal. I was brought in to see him: as his subordinate, he did not deem me worthy of sitting in the administration's armchairs. After a few brief questions, heavy silence for three full minutes. Clearly, the venerable old man was searching his brain for a compliment that whole time, as one has the habit of doing to the natives. In fact, the subsequent events confirmed my supposition. The acting governor asked me, in the event that I were to be accepted at Saint-Cyr, when I planned to enroll. And I, like a good little boy, tried to explain it to him: I told him that admission to the school did not take place on the same day for everyone; that it was done by intervals of approximately eight days; that those who placed first in their exams entered last and those who placed last entered first.

"So, my friend," Mr. Ballay said to me, his fat face beaming, "I believe in that case you can prepare yourself to be among those who will be admitted first at Saint-Cyr."

I tell you; Mr. Ballay dearly misled me because I was not accepted at Saint-Cyr; otherwise, his compliment was well deserved, but hell, I should have known I was too vain thinking that a Black man could be accepted at one of the best schools in France. Thus, I was not at all surprised by his excessive courtesy. Besides, Mr. Ballay would have broken the custom of African civil servants had he spoken to me any differently. I took leave quite humbly, content to simply ask that Mr. Delvaux reimburse me for my railway fare, which, by the way, he neither accepted nor refused. I spent forty-nine francs. They gave me back thirty-nine francs and thirty-five centimes: my goodness, that outcome was so unexpected I had to thank God.

All that pettiness had left me more or less indifferent, but my real torment began on September 6th in the evening.

I was supposed to embark on the 7th in the afternoon: I had been in bed for exactly forty minutes when at midnight someone knocked on my door. I stumbled out of bed and went to open the door for my nocturnal visitor and found myself face to face with a European man wearing a large hood, which completely prevented me from knowing what social class he belonged to, whether a civilian or in the military. What was also even odder about him, was that he would neither come in nor tell me his name. It was impossible for me to get anything out of him at all: all he told me was that he knew you, that he had seen me with you in 1890 and on other occasions in France, that he had followed me in my studies and knew of the success I had achieved, and, finally, that he was fascinated by me. He told me that it was because of all those various reasons that he took the liberty to come find me and give me a friendly piece of advice. Here is what resulted from our exchange.

The man: You are still quite young, son, and wherever you go you need to be accompanied, someone to look after you. I do not blame you at all for coming to see your mother. To the contrary, it is a very natural feeling on your part, which does you honor. Except that you have chosen to do this at a bad time, I believe. From what I can tell, the people under whose command you are here are not very well inclined toward you.

Me: But sir, why would those people of whom you speak be disinclined toward me? They do not even know me: I am in no way hindering their affairs or ambitions, given that I do not have a very enviable social position. It is thus intolerable that anyone should wish me any harm.

The man: My poor child, your reasoning is that of a decent man, but unfortunately no one fits into that category anymore. People who are mean do not need to know someone to do them harm and, believe me, it is never without a purpose, an interest . . . and well, you may not even realize what they want from you, but whatever it may be, try to use what I am going to tell you to your advantage.

You are going to leave tomorrow; in addition to a few Europeans who are leaving, you will be in the company of three Black men who will be in first class, which is unheard of since even the viceroys travel in second class. You have nothing to worry about with the one named Abdoulaye Seck. He is a brave telegraphist taking leave in Bamako. But be wary of the other two: the Wolof man, Ali, who is a bit up there in age and a little mean . . . his mission is to surveil your rapport with the Black people during the trip. The young Toucouleur, Ticiré, in whom you will undoubtedly have more confidence because of his race, is charged with the task of engaging you in conversations that are completely opposed to the interests of France. He is to worm it out of you, as the popular expression goes, and he will invent as needed. Moreover, they are known for their nefarious work. All the natives know those two; even the Whites know them.'

Farewell, young friend, try to use what you know to your advantage, and perhaps one day you will return the favor to me.

Then we parted ways.

It goes without saying that was a sleepless night for me.

The next day, September 7th, I departed; and with mathematical precision, everything that individual had predicted occurred like clockwork. But, fortunately for me, luck was on my side: aided by Mr. Pierron, whom you must know, some other Europeans who were on board, as well as our imbecile spies, after three days, the mystery was solved. Ticiré dared to ask Abdoulaye Seck to provide him a report. The latter sent the auxiliary interpreter because Ticiré has that title. He came to find me, told me the story, and showed his service book to one of the Europeans so they did not confuse him with the people of that infamous gang.

In Kayes, the two snitches hung around outside my house, but I promise you that I dealt the young Toucouleur man something he will remember for the rest of his life, which he will never boast about. Then I found out, from a European, about the intimate relationships my two men had with Samba Ibrahim, former interpreter, now director of the School for Hostages in Kayes. What's more, during my stay in Kayes, every time I went to visit the European quarter, I always bumped into Samba Ibrahim along my way.

Now, I will explain the rest of my journey to you.

Naturally, on my return trip, I traveled with my spies from Kayes to Saint-Louis.

Now, let's back up a little: we arrived in Kayes on September 18th around seven o'clock in the morning; as soon as they dropped anchor, I disembarked and waited calmly for an hour because I figured they would have sent at least one duty officer to tell me what I was supposed to do. Since I didn't see anyone, I went to the district commander in Kayes who, for the first day, deemed it appropriate to be somewhat polite. There, I was offered a chair, to my surprise, and told to wait [...].

At nine o'clock, I was in the military staff offices. I introduced myself to Captain Morisson who brought me in to see Captain Ballieux and, accompanied by two officers, I went up to Lieutenant-Colonel Lamory's residence. I mixed up my greetings before I crossed the threshold of the office of this eminent person. Every response was brief, dry. A real truly authoritative tone. Then the real interrogation began.

Mr. Lamory: Take a seat, sit down, and answer the questions I am going to ask you.

Me: Yes, Colonel.

Mr. Lamory: When did you arrive?

Me: This morning, at 7AM, Colonel.

Mr. Lamory: When did you leave France?

Me: Colonel, I...

Mr. Lamory: Quiet. (Silence.) Hmm... Yes... Yes, that's right: when did you leave France? (Silence again.) Uh yes, would you please do me the honor of responding?

Me: I left Bordeaux August 27th on the transatlantic liner Le Brésil and arrived in Dakar on September 4th.

Mr. Lamory: Oh, that is terrific... yes, yes, what are people f... doing in this ministry? We do not even know dates anymore. I was sent a telegram saying you were leaving France on October 8th and here you are in front of me now.

Me: Colonel, I have nothing to do with the mistaken dates. Surely, they meant that I was supposed to leave again from Dakar on October 7th to return to France.

Mr. Lamory: But when someone tells you something, are you even capable of handling your responsibility?

Me: But, Colonel, I meant that...

Mr. Lamory: Quiet. You were given five hundred francs, correct? What did you do with that money?

Me: Four years ago, Colonel, when I received permission from Mr. Bontemps to go see my mother, he asked me to give him a list of items I...

Mr. Lamory: What? What is this story you are telling me? Stick to the point.

Me: But, Colonel, knowing what happened four years ago is essential for understanding how I spent the five hundred francs I was given.

Mr. Lamory: Hmm... yes... yes, that's fine, you can leave now. Do not incur any debts, do not acquire any wives, and set a good example in the colony. Hmm, yes, well yes... come back to see me again before you leave.

Thinking that my interrogation had ended, I was about to walk out when a booming "hey!" rooted me to my chair.

Mr. Lamory: What was your situation four years ago?

Me: When I went on my first trip, Colonel Bonnier was in Kayes: before I arrived, he had given my mother some money so she could buy the things she needed during her stay. Every day he had a ration of rice and meat given to my mother and her people. As for me, I had an officer's ration, a cook, a boy, a horse and a stableman. Samba Ibrahim managed my cook's expenses.

Mr. Lamory: Yes, son, all that is very well, but I am

not required to do what was done four years ago. Times change, you see. Samba Ibrahim will deal with you.

They had an orderly bring me to my mother's. After searching for an hour, because the poor kid did not know where my family was, we finally arrived.

I spent three days in Kayes with no bed, no food, no boy, and I only got a fork and knife on the fifth day.

Since Captain Morisson had told me that I would get everything by the evening of September 18th, after two days of all that, I went back to his office to explain my predicament.

"So go see Samba Ibrahim," he told me, "He has orders for that."

I went to see Samba. He sent me back to the military staff, they sent me back to him again. I knew they were making fun of me, so I accepted it, which was, after all, the wisest thing to do.

Luckily for me, I am not too fussy and was able to easily reaccustom myself with the way of life there.

On my fifth day there, my sister who was in Fakola, near Medina, on the right bank of the Senegal River, had come to Kayes with her children, her husband and some slaves she had been athorized to keep, since many had been taken from her a while before that. My mother, lacking resources to feed so many people that were around her, decided to inform me of her situa-

tion and told me that six days before I had arrived in Kayes she had gone to see Mr. Lamory to ask him if he intended to treat her like Colonel Bonnier had, explaining to him that she was in the same financial situation in Kayes as she had been four years earlier, in other words that she was not home and had no way to support herself in this place.

So, Mr. Lamory replied that his job there was not to feed my family. My poor mother went home, having been excited to see me arrive, thinking that he might have a little more consideration for me.

Naturally, before trying a new approach with the governor, I started buying millet, rice, three blankets and native beds while I still had some money left. After that, I went up to the government office: Captain Morisson, the director of political affairs, whom I saw first, sent me to Captain Ballieux, the director of native affairs. I asked him if I could see Mr. Lamory. Of course, since my problems were not important enough to disturb an acting governor, he told me to explain the purpose of my visit to him, which I did rhapsodically, trying to soften his heart of stone by telling him all about my poor mother's situation.

Captain Ballieux was a tall man, very tall indeed, and thin, with a dry personality. His head sat perpendicularly on his neck, and when he spoke to his inferiors, his eyes were imbued with extraordinary insolence.

Looking at me squarely in the eye, he replied to all my requests with: "That has nothing to do with me. I couldn't give a f... You were given five hundred francs. Deal with it." He still ended up promising to be my interpreter with Mr. Lamory, though, and told me to come back the following day.

The following day I went back, and, to my great deception, I found out that the colonel had made a decision regarding my request, in other words: I should not expect anything from him during my stay. As I was leaving, I learned something else that is very upsetting. I found it outrageous even, because it damaged my reputation. The acting governor had warned the merchants to be wary of me: that anywhere I went to buy something, they needed to make me pay in cash. Otherwise, the goods delivered to me would be lost.

Fortunately for me, during the first few days I was there, I had been able to earn the trust of a few good Frenchmen who, aware of the difficulties I was up against, were willing to help me.

On my thirteenth day in Kayes, all that remained of my blessed five hundred francs was one centime. Again, I went to see Mr. Ballieux. "I would love to bore the colonel once again with your request," he said to me, "but admit it, this is getting old, isn't it? Come back tomorrow."

The next day, just like the day following my first

request, was one of blighted hope for me. Mr. Ballieux told me that Mr. Lamory recognized that he had been wrong about me, but that he had made a decision which he could not go back on. That was no consolation for someone asking for bread.

Thanks to the Blacks, some of whom brought me millet, milk, and others meat, kola and even food that was fully prepared, I was able to hold out until October 4th.

After that date, believing I would be staying a few more days, I decided to make one last effort with the person who, in my eyes, represented France. Through Samba Ibrahim, I was given either three francs and seventy centimes or three francs and seventy-five centimes per day. I wanted them to give me three or four days-worth at a time so that I could buy enough millet: a bag of coarse millet costs seven francs and fifty centimes. So, I went to the government offices: it goes without saying that I did not see Mr. Lamory. Captain Ballieux whom I spoke with once again told me I was stubborn and annoying and that, furthermore, what I was asking for was trafficking, unworthy of a soldier and therefore I must leave him alone.

So then, since I did not want my mother to know the truth about her situation, which might have made everything worse, I went back to my new friends. One of them sent me a bag of millet and a voucher for a bag of corn. Since it was October 7ᵗʰ and I knew, even though the governor had not deemed it worth notifying me, that I would be leaving soon, I saved the voucher for the corn and am sending it to you. It is living proof of the way I have been treated in the French Sudan.

On October 7ᵗʰ, in the evening, I was called to the governor's office. So, I went. Captain Ballieux gave me a piece of paper which said that throughout my stay I had been fostered at the colony's expense, and that, during the rest of my time in Saint-Louis and Dakar, I would receive compensation of ten francs per day, to the exclusion of any other sum. I pointed out to him that I had absolutely no money, that I was leaving my family behind in Kayes and that, furthermore, living in Saint-Louis and Dakar would certainly cost more than ten francs per day. To which he replied: "I couldn't give a f... That has nothing to do with me. You were given five hundred francs and, anyway, now you're going to be dealing with the colonel." We went up to Mr. Lamory's office, and here is what he said.

"Take a seat, sit down and listen to me. Hmm, yes, hmm, yes, yes ... oh yes, aren't you handsome, very handsome. That is your pride, what goes to your head: Aren't you the one who said you would be much better off in Germany than in France, that in the Sudan there were only morons, that the soldiers were mere brag-

garts, and that the little good that had been done in the country was thanks to civilians? Ah yes . . . that's nice, very nice. But be careful! You are not in France yet, and we could be your masters. Yes, and he wants to be admitted to Saint-Cyr, yes, yes, I do not need to tell you that you would make a sad officer, an unworthy officer. After all, we have the right to treat you as we wish. You are merely the son of a vanquished man."

To which I replied: "Colonel, sir, I have absolutely nothing to say to you: I will not swear before the great Gods, nor will I try to defend myself. You clearly have a very strong opinion about me; perhaps one needs to have such a rapport with me."

I was ordered to leave, which I did swiftly since being in the presence of such people made me deeply disgusted. On my way out, I met Captain Morisson who handed me two letters from Mr. de l'Isle de Sales, one of which had been opened: about which I received neither an explanation nor an excuse. What boorishness, my God!

Would you even think me capable, dear General, of saying the things Mr. Lamory accuses me of? Nonetheless, since they have attributed such words to me, I accept them and will add that:

Most of the officers who are sent to the French Sudan to serve their homeland are unworthy of the mission with which they are entrusted: even those who start out with honorable and humanitarian intentions become very quickly corrupted by the mere contact with those whom alcohol has stupefied. Concerned [. . .] with covering their sleeves with stripes and their chests with honorary badges, all they are good at is starting wars. And if there are no wars, they just massacre the poor Blacks whom they push into war, through atrocities. And then, since they are the winners, they aggrieve the women and torture the defenseless children.

Those are the good effects of this civilization whose name is invoked each time the need arises.

Now, as for the intentional insult that Mr. Lamory uttered to me, I also accept it: he is right. I am merely the son of a vanquished man and as such I should only expect humiliation and crudeness from brutes like him. I am the son of a vanquished man, that is true, but I am pleased to point out that Mr. Lamory is the only one, out of all the French people, who reminded me of what my life was like in France. In any case, he was not the one who conquered my father, and the person who did knew—due to, through his good will and through his affection—how to make his son forget that he had been deprived of his father and family. In any event, I hope that God, the supporter of the weak and father of orphans, will help me and that one day, despite my status as the vanquished sultan, I will be able to ask Mr. Lamory the reason for his insolence.

I left Kayes again on October 8th in the evening, leaving my family without a penny. We arrived in Saint-Louis on the 12th at seven thirty in the morning. I had barely disembarked and by eight thirty, I was with Mr. Delvaux. I explained to him how impossible it would be for me to find a hotel in Saint-Louis for less than ten francs a night; I implored him to help me, to either pay the balance of what I would be lacking or lodge me in the barracks. As you can see, there was nothing extravagant about my request. But despite that, I heard the same old story, which I was beginning to know by heart: "You were given five hundred francs, now deal with it." "On the other hand," Mr. Delvaux added, "the governor of the French Sudan wrote that you would receive ten francs per day, to the exclusion of any other sum. Therefore, we cannot give anything beyond that." That was when Mr. Chaudié came in. I greeted him, exited the office, and stood there for a moment just outside the door because I was hoping that his arrival would perhaps help my situation.

Alas! Again, another error on my part. Mr. Chaudié stayed for about twenty minutes then went quietly back upstairs. It was only at ten o'clock that Mr. Delvaux noticed I was still at the door. He told me to go inside, sort out my papers and come back to him with an answer. I got back around ten thirty. I informed him that I was only to receive forty francs since I was taking the ocean liner on October 16th. The information I gave him had absolutely no effect on him, and he sent me walking.

I did not consider myself beaten because, not having any time to lose, I had decided to return to the office that same evening. While I waited, I went down to the Chanfrein Hotel. On the 13th in the morning, I went to the residence again, though I was convinced that the outcome would not be any better than the previous day. I had barely arrived, and Mr. Delvaux offered me some "good advice": to leave without paying. "Thank you, Sir," I replied to him, saying that "whereas dishonesty was accepted in Senegalese customs, unfortunately for me, I was not raised with such principles; if I cannot pay what I owe, I will leave my trunk, or else, since you want me to manage on my own so badly, well, I will comply with your orders."

Faced with such determination on my part, determination that he certainly understood, he told me to come back on the 14th.

On that date, with the payment order in hand, which I had received inside and which, consequently, proved that I was only to receive forty francs, I went back to find Mr. Delvaux. He gave me a total of fifty francs, after which he asked me to go up to the governor's office.

"I have here," Mr. Chaudié told me, "a letter from Mr. Lamory: he is quite displeased with you and informs me that your conduct in Kayes was deplor-

able, and that you have absolutely failed the officers. Watch yourself, or else I will forbid you to remain in my colonies."

"I understand, Mr. Governor," I replied, "Mr. Lamory has already made me aware of his displeasure with me. But I admit that I do not at all understand the expression 'failed the officers,' just as I cannot fathom the suspicious conduct in which I engaged in Kayes."

He ended our conversation with that timeless phrase people turn to when they simply do not know what to respond to the questions they are asked: "That'll do."

On the 16th I boarded the ocean liner La Guinée in Dakar and arrived in Paris (October 30th) wanting only to go to bed: the trip had tired me out so much that I was coming down with bronchitis.

Despite that, I was so eager to know where I stood that on Wednesday, November 3rd, I presented myself at the Ministry of the Colonies, in the company of Mr. de l'Isle de Sales. Of course, Mr. Binger began by pointing out that I was wrong. When I informed him about the way that I had been treated, he seemed a little shaken and asked Mr. de l'Isle de Sales to come back in the afternoon so that he could see the report they had on my misconduct. I am sending you the summary of that report here, but it is to be kept strictly confidential since Mr. Binger provided us with the information as a *friend rather than officially.*

There are two categories of accusations against me: the first being things I allegedly said:

1) On the boat: that I had influential friends (journalists) and that I knew how to use them to my advantage; that Abd el-Kader's grandchildren would no longer receive their boarding pension but that I knew how to get that for myself.

2) That Aguibou, his son and the other kings were nothing since they could not order people's heads to be cut off; that when I earned my stripes, I would be omnipotent.

3) That I would be better off in Germany than in France.

My actions, for which they are accusing me:

1) For forbidding old Oussoubé (one of your former cooks whom I stayed with) to close the door to the house at night so I could invite questionable people in, and that I did so violently.

2) For having my own court and for having Blacks follow me at a distance through the streets.

3) For liking to spend money.

4) For putting officers on a pedestal.

Conclusion: it would be dangerous if I were to become an officer.

If you please, my dear General, I would like to reply in detail to each of those items.

> *1) The first issue seems so idiotic to me it would be useless to discuss it: I ascribe it to the weakening mental state of the author of the report.*
>
> *2) I would be a fool and a terrible liar if I did not recognize the omnipotence of the Sudanese viceroys: on the contrary, those little despots are Genghis Khans, [...]. I will just take one as an example: Mademba, the figure to whom I will do this honor, an honor which, moreover, is rightfully his, because he represents the true type of those tyrannical kinglets. Since he has been in power, he has cut off the heads of more than forty-seven people; and since he is morally and physically weary, he is constantly telling those who displease him: "You do not know what royalty is! If you do not stop, I will bash in your head, and you will die." [...]*

I purposely used Mademba as an example, because I myself have reason to complain about him; One of my sisters, Diaïnabou Oumou, is at his residence; all he does is insult her, hit her and even shackle her. Of course, I do not hate Mademba. I even forgive him because I understand that he makes her withstand what he cannot do to her father: that is what makes cowards, truly depraved souls. Oh, how happy he must be, that man who, having emerged from the dregs of Saint-Louis society, achieved the kind of power he never would have dared to dream! What glory for him to have one of El Hadj Oumar's granddaughters in his loathsome harem!

3) The topic of Germany is as puerile as the first, however I will stop there for a moment. I have never spoken about Germany in any way, neither good nor bad, and if I had done so, I would not have taken the Sudanese as my confidants for the very simple reason that they do not even know that the German people exist. What I understand from all of that, quite clearly, is that they want me to imagine living in a country other than France.

4) If what they mean by having a court is having people who used to bring me rice, millet, milk, kolas, and meat . . . if what they mean by a court are those who I welcomed into my home, yes, I admit that I had one and that, on those rare occasions that I even went out, some Blacks did follow me at a distance. It is a moment of forgetfulness on my part, because I should have remembered that as the son of a vanquished man, I did not have the right to act as an individual. Except that, four years ago, Mr. Bonnier did not see any risk in that.

5) In fact, I did tell Oussoubé, who closed the door

at eight o'clock, to leave the key with one of my mother's captives who slept in the boulo (an anteroom of the house), since he had a lot of difficulty getting up to open the door for me when I came home. I do not in any way regret that incident, because it is not a crime to delight in some amusement at my age. That little fact which seems insignificant in and of itself was largely about Mr. Lamory's indisposition toward me. Unbeknownst to me, my nocturnal outings disturbed the acting governor's habits, and consequently I find it completely natural for him to seek revenge.

6) It is said that I like to spend money. That seems impossible to me. Even if I admitted to that, I certainly could not have developed such habits with the little money the government gave me.

7) As for the officers, I do not know how I could have offended them, since I had no relationship with any of them except Captains Morisson and Ballieux with whom I was always on my best behavior despite the latter's rudeness.

Now that I have made known to you, at length, almost day by day, all the adventures of my journey, it is important, my dear General, that you recognize my determination.

"As true as God alone is God [...] whoever, out of malice or out of interest (I admit with difficulty this

latter hypothesis), will prevent me from achieving the goal I have set for myself, I swear before God who alone can see into the depths of my soul, that he will have my life, and I will have his."

I am very aware of my situation: my only crime is being the son of Ahmadou and having been brought back to France by you; but I am proud of the first and I will try to make myself worthy of the second. What they want is to push me to act on some sudden impulse and afterward, they will place the blame on someone: 'Yes,' they will say, 'what was the need to have this little Black boy brought to France?'"

TO REMAIN FRENCH

FRÉJUS, FRANCE, CENTER FOR THE HISTORICAL STUDY OF OVERSEAS TROOPS

I reread the entire last sentence: "What they want is to push me to act on some sudden impulse and afterward, they will place the blame on someone: 'Yes' they will say, 'what was the need to have this little Black boy brought to France?'"

I had the odd impression that nothing had changed after one hundred twenty years, that the scenes that were playing out in 1897 in the governor's office in Kayes or in Saint-Louis were repeating themselves today in the French police stations, with on the one hand the conviction of some that might is right, and on the other, proof that one must remain patient and calm, not act on a sudden impulse, whether one are is right or wrong. I had a better understanding of the "misguidedness" for which the administration had reproached Abdoulaye—the idea was not to forgive the person who pointed out the injustice of the situation. Not then, not now.

I thought of Assa Traoré's struggle to obtain the truth for her brother Adama, who died while in police custody in France in 2016.

I thought of the death of George Floyd in the United States in May 2020, about how his death had sparked demonstrations on both sides of the Atlantic. "Black Lives Matter," they said. I thought about that week in June when, in several European countries, statues had fallen or been defaced. On Saturday, June 6th, in Paris, demonstrators had sprayed red paint on the statue of Colbert, Louis XIV's Minister of State, architect of the Code Noir who drafted legislation concerning slaves. That same weekend in June, the statue of slave trader Edward Colston had been thrown into the water in Bristol, England. The following Monday, the statue of Henry Dundas—who had campaigned against the abolition of slavery—had been covered in graffiti in Edinburgh, Scotland. On Tuesday, a statue of King Leopold II, known for his tyrannical reign over Congo, had been toppled in a park in Anvers, Belgium. The same day, the mayor of London, Sadiq Khan, decided to remove the statue of slave trader Robert Milligan, while at Oxford demonstrators were demanding that the one of Cecil Rhodes, Prime Minister of the Cape, be taken down. If slavery were the most brutal manifestation of this domination, there was another, more pernicious one, the knowledge of absolute power and our imprisoned gazes, a legacy that one hundred years were perhaps not enough to change.

I read and reread the eleven pages of that letter filled with the cold anger of that young man who claimed to be equally French and African, at once Ahmadou's son and Archinard's godson. There was no place for him in the world in which he had been born. Archinard had dreamed of the impossible: a Black French citizen. And if Abdoulaye had achieved that, he was suddenly brought to heel. At the top of the last page was a new date. Abdoulaye had spent several days writing his letter, and he had finished it on December 9, 1897. The tone was less oppositional. The young man shared news of two of his classmates who had been accepted to Saint-Cyr. He also thanked Archinard for the photo he had sent him. He included a "detailed memorandum for the unforgettable five hundred francs" which listed all expenses incurred, including in total about five hundred yards of various fabrics and small bottles of perfumes and cologne. Abdoulaye had decided to pamper his family. You just did not come back empty-handed after being away for four years, no more in 1897 than you would today.

I had five more letters to read. In the one from December 31, 1897, written only a few weeks later, Abdoulaye was angry again. All that traveling was starting to take a toll on him. For the first time, his words revealed anger toward Archinard for the control he had wielded over the young man's life.

> *If it is enough to work hard, be patient and even suffer in silence to conserve your affection for the son of a vanquished man, well, I believe I have. However, do not ignore that I am only a child, that human nature*

is full of weaknesses and that the strongest among us often find it quite difficult to resign themselves. [. . .] I know now what kind of vileness the people under whose authority I have been placed are capable of. They have a child come to France, without having consulted him or his parents. Then, because a drunkard filed a complaint against him, his career was destroyed without anyone deigning to hear his side. Unsatisfied with that, they want to rip him away from the new family that formed around him, of his new friends who made him forget his old friends and the past. Unsatisfied with that, since they cannot strangle him in broad daylight, they want to send him to some far-off land where no one will be able to hear him while his executioners finish the job.

His anger was no longer cold. It had turned into rage and revolt.

Fortunately for me, and unfortunately for those who want to send me to die in Madagascar, I found a few good and loyal French men who have always taken an interest in me and who, even in this iniquity, assure me of their support for me. It is a clever idea to want to have me go to Madagascar: Mr. Gallieni, who maneuvers his gun so well and who must still remember the way he was treated by my father during his captivity, will certainly

*find some pretext to lodge those two bullets in my head
that a certain Jean Le Breil editor at* La Dépêche *colonial, finds essential for peace in Senegal and Sudan.*

What did Archinard think about all that, as he was receiving Abdoulaye's letters in Cochinchina? In February 1898, he wrote a long memorandum to the Minister of Colonies, the draft of which was slipped in between the letters he had received from Abdoulaye. In it, he defended the young man and recalled his story. He recounted Abdoulaye's first days in Paris, perhaps to show how far he had come since then.

Having arrived in Paris and having only a few days to spend in France before returning to the Sudan, I tried to rid myself as swiftly as possible of Abdou Lahi who was at the time quite troublesome to me because of his savagery and stubbornness in preserving the customs and traditional dress from Ségou. [. . .] At the beginning of his stay in Paris, he was treated a bit like a spoilt child and was invited to various ministries and official functions, and he received quite a number of small gifts [. . .] When I came to France, I found he had become quite the little Parisian.

I thought again about that eleven-year-old child on his tricycle, letting go of his habits little by little, but continuing to sign his name in two alphabets, each time recalling his filiation, his father's name, like a pride he had never relinquished, but which ended up being reduced to an insult with that form of address he was forced to endure on his second trip: "son of the vanquished Sultan Ahmadou".

Archinard argued at length for Abdoulaye to be admitted to Saint-Cyr, always with the idea that such an education could only reinforce his usefulness in the service to the colonial troops. He did not let up on his plan.

That year, 1898, Abdoulaye wrote several letters to Archinard, in March, in July, in September and in October. It was a year of struggle trying to get him registered at Saint-Cyr, after completing a second year of preparation at Janson-de-Sailly High School.

> *As for me, Abdoulaye wrote in July, my intention is to continue at Saint-Cyr. Mr. de l'Isle de Sales is going to take the necessary steps to have me admitted as a native (and not as a foreigner) and promises I will be naturalized when I am of legal age to be able to serve in a regiment garrisoned in the metropole.*

But Abdoulaye's grades were not good enough, and one of his teachers ended up advising him to abandon the competitive examination track.

> *Some examiners, he wrote in September, claim that I am usurping a spot, since I do not take German like*

everyone else, and that I believe I will be admitted to Saint-Cyr without having to pass the exams. On the other hand, those allegations were nearly confirmed officially to Mr. de l'Isle de Sales. You must understand if I show fear at the prospect of being "rejected" indefinitely. It is so easy to "flunk" a candidate.

It was at that time that the ministry received the letters from the journalist Henri des Houx, from Mr. de l'Isle de Sales, and the one from Abdoulaye in which he affirmed his attachment to his "adopted homeland," those letters that I read in the archives of Aix-en-Provence. That was when the conditions were established: two years of service in the foreign Legion. Then, in October, came the decision from the ministry confirming his admission, the telegram announcing the date of his aptitude examination. The following day, Abdoulaye added a post-scriptum to the letter he had started earlier, and which was the last trace that I could find of him in the archives: "Everything worked out. Mr. de l'Isle de Sales saw General Maillard, the commander of the school, who was absolutely charming, in my opinion. I was admitted to Saint-Cyr on Monday, October 31st."

Abdoulaye's voice died there. I returned the last crate and went outside among the blooming mimosas. As I walked along the road toward a bus stop further down, I passed in front of a dark ocher mosque. It looked like the ancient mosques of West Africa, like those in Djenné, Mali or Agadez,

Niger. It looked as if it were abandoned, surrounded by a fence. As I searched for information about that building that had appeared out of nowhere, standing there amidst the parasol pines, opposite a primary school, I discovered a part of Fréjus's history that I had not suspected, which was linked to that of the Senegalese riflemen, those soldiers of the colonial army from all over French West Africa, who were recruited en masse during World War I to fight in Europe. They had landed in Fréjus where a camp had been set up for acclimatization and transit. Some had died there. There are still some tombs of those soldiers in the municipal cemetery. The camp was in that part of the city where the Marine Troops Museum and the Center for the Historical Study of Overseas Troops were located from then onwards. The Missiri Mosque had been built after the war, in 1930, for those riflemen who had continued to serve in the colonial troops outside of Africa.

At the end of the day, walking along the seashore, I came upon a monument honoring the black soldiers who had died during the First World I. It depicted a group of several human-sized figures, one carrying an injured soldier, another with a flag in his hand, and a third gazing up at the sky. Engraved on a plaque was a quote by poet and first President of independent Senegal, Léopold Sédar Senghor, himself a veteran of the Second World War: "Passersby, they fell, fraternally united, so that you could remain French."

It reminded me of Abdoulaye and his dream of becoming an officer. I thought about what I knew about another descendant of El Hadj Oumar Tall, his grandson Thierno Seydou Nourou Tall, who was said to have been born the year his grandfather died, which would be 1864, though sources did not really confirm it. One thing was certain, however: Thierno Seydou Nourou Tall was one of the great caliphs of the Oumar Tall family, a respected figure and mediator. He was the one who had given his blessing to the young Mamadou Ly, when he was leaving for France where the latter would find the objects from the Natural History Museum of Le Havre.

During the First World War, when the French needed to recruit troops in their colonies, the French governor entrusted the task to Blaise Diagne, the first African deputy elected to the French Chamber of Deputies. Born in Gorée, Senegal, and familiar with his country, Diagne went first to the religious leaders of the different brotherhoods to try to convince them. Each of the latter, to give an example, sent one of their sons to the front and thus served as intermediaries in their recruitment. That is how, only fifteen years after Abdoulaye's death, having tried so hard to get into a French military school, then simply dying of tuberculosis, one of his cousins, Thierno Seydou Nourou Tall, ended up recruiting riflemen to go fight alongside the French. There is something ironic about history.

"ALL I HAVE ARE HYPOTHESES, NOTHING IS CERTAIN"

PARIS, FRANCE
THE ARMY MUSEUM

Sabers, swords and daggers. Gladiator swords, spears and blades. The display cases in the hall leading to the 17th and 18th century rooms of The Army Museum at Les Invalides in Paris were a parade of bladed weapons, manufactured in the factories of Versailles, Maubeuge, Châtellerault and often, very often, in the Klingenthal factory, as was the case of the saber blade that was "returned" to Senegal. For me, that name was since associated with that of El Hadj Oumar Tall. One no longer went without the other. My research had traced in my mind a shortcut between an ancient royal factory in Alsace and a leader of holy wars who had left the banks of the Senegal River—even though, during my two years of research, my doubts about the reality of the historical connection between those two names had only multiplied. I looked at the sabers, blades and swords from Klingenthal, which were in nearly every display case. I stopped to count them and smiled: I had gotten caught up in my own game.

The previous day, I had consulted the only written proof I had found in the museum archives that connected El Hadj Oumar Tall to the saber that Édouard Philippe had "returned": a letter written by Archinard, addressed to the director of the museum, General Niox. The archivist had taken out the file for me—there were neither boxes nor crates. The traces Archinard had left consisted of five letters, all dated April 1909, linked to objects donated to the museum. The saber was mentioned in the first letter, written on April 3, 1909.

Archinard began his letter by listing seventeen objects that had come from four different battles which he wanted to donate to the museum. There were, first, objects from Ségou: parts of harnesses that Archinard attributed to "Ahmadou, El Hadj Oumar's son," namely a chest, three head pieces, two bridles, two attachment collars, two bits and a pair of spurs (were those the pieces that had arrived at the same time as the jewelry of which I had found no trace?). Next were objects attributed to Madani, "Ahmadou's son and delegated successor": a pair of boots and a Toucouleur hat. Then, seized at the "Battle of Gouri, the last fight against Ahmadou," a "ceremonial axe which was carried ahead of Ahmadou during the ceremonies, and which had been picked up off the battlefield". Finally, there was a war boubou "covered with gris-gris or talismans that belonged to one of Samory's warriors," recovered during the fighting around Kankan, "one of Samory's capitals."

The saber was mentioned on the second page of the letter, under the title "Siege of Bandiagara":

"Saber having belonged to El Hadj Oumar. The blade must not have been drawn from its sheath afterward by anyone but he himself. The saber was rejoined with the sheath by a leather braid which I cut."

The saber from the museum, the one that had been on loan to Senegal on three separate occasions, then "returned" by Édouard Philippe in November 2019 therefore had nothing to do with the one that had been taken in Ségou and inventoried among the crates that had left Kayes in September 1890, then exhibited in February 1893 at the Permanent Exhibition of the Colonies. That same saber I had found traces of in the archives in Aix-en-Provence and in the press of the time. That explained why the description of the object in an article from 1893 did not correspond with the weapon that had since been on exhibit at the Museum of Black Civilizations in Dakar. Moreover, the siege of Bandiagara only took place at the end of April of 1893 . . . in other words more than two months after the exhibition in Paris had opened. It was therefore impossible that it was the same object—unless Archinard had lied about the origin of his donation.

In the four letters that followed, in response to General Niox's request, Archinard gave additional information about the battles, but said nothing else about the saber. He took the opportunity, however, to add dozens of new pieces to the list of donations, as if he had been seized by a sudden burst of generosity.

There he recorded a saber (another one! Though that one was not attributed to any illustrious figure), a cap, a powder horn, a dagger and a belt "having belonged to Boukar, a Sopha chief, commander in Koundian for Ahmadou," slaves' iron shackles and donkey fetters, a "two-handed saber with a blade from Spain labeled Dona Maria" (out of three!) from Dougoura's battle against Samory, as well as a copper-plated ceremonial cane, a fly swatter made of an elephant tail and a hat that had belonged to one of Ahmadou's griots from Ségou, a silver bracelet from the "Treasure of Ségou," a pair of razors that had belonged to one of Ahmadou's wives, and a meticulously described Tijani rite rosary: "silver inlaid ebony beads with separation pieces made of small braided leather straps, having belonged to Ahmadou (no native work is finer or more detailed)."

There was also a silver medal and "a bag that belonged to one of Ahmadou's Toucouleur horsemen killed during combat (knife, needle holder, pliers for removing thorns, gris-gris or talismans against bullets, against saber blows, against illness, against thieves, against women's infidelities, and for the horse's longevity and good health)," taken at the time of the battle of Kalé fought by Captain Ruault against Ahmadou's troops on June 3, 1890. From the battles of Niogoméra and Korriga, carried out in October 1890, again against Ahmadou's troops, the general brought back a silver Koran box "having belonged to Ali Bouri, one of Ahmadou's most faithful disciples." Taken at Nioro on January 1, 1891: "a stone from the fortress wall built by El Hadj Oumar in the city center." Taken from Diéna on February 4, 1891: two quivers and some poison arrows, two bows and a wrist pad, a bamboo poison container, and three native bullets "two of which were fired at me, one missed, the other penetrated my horse's neck outside of Diéna." Regarding the third, Archinard gave the following account:

> *[It] was found inside the body of a chicken amongst those which various villagers had offered to me alive as a sign of their submission. According to our natives, they would have made the chicken swallow the bullet which would have poisoned it with the intention of poisoning me. We ate the chicken and experienced no ailment.*

The list of objects went on for several pages. Archinard seemed to take pleasure in doing so, providing more and more detail. Taken from Daba by Colonel Desbordes on January 16, 1883: a bracelet decorated with two cowries and three rings, a bell and a small gong. The battles at Ouégako in April 1883: a native armchair.

Then moving on to the gifts Archinard received: a powder horn inlaid with silver, given to him by Aguibou, Ahmadou's brother, an ally of the French. A small bronze statue "cast by the natives of the French Sudan [...] which represented a squad of riflemen in chechias, rifles slung over their shoulders, accompanied by a European sergeant."

At times, Archinard doubted the origin of the objects. That is how he wrote about a "bisac de cheval": "originates from the siege of Ségou or was sent to me while I was in Sudan—I can no longer be certain—but I believe we can place it with the objects originating from Ségou."

The abundance of objects was overwhelming. It was a frenzied feeling as if at a garage sale or a moving sale, as if there were suddenly a need to get rid of things that are burdensome.

The general ended his letter by stating: "Tomorrow, I will send you my new notes and additional items. I need you to give me a few days. I have a lot of work now at the army corps with the mobilization."

Within two weeks, Archinard had listed sixty-nine objects that he donated to the museum, among which was "El Hadj Oumar's saber." And the general did not intend to stop there.

> *I will likely have a few more little things to give to you, he wrote at the end of his last letter, for instance javelin irons in the shape of a rosette, which Dr. Collomb extracted from our wounded in Djenné, but I definitely will not be able to do it for a while—I would have to move some trunks to the countryside and do not have time to do that now.*

We had to wait until 2020 for Lucile Paraponaris, the person in charge of research from the Army Museum who had been hired at the beginning of that year for a newly created position, to find those letters again. Her first task was to index all the African objects in the collection as there were around two thousand two hundred of them among the five hundred thousand pieces in the museum. Then she had to retrace the journey of the "saber said to have belonged to El Hadj Oumar," the label that would be used thenceforth from then on to refer to that object.

When Lucile Paraponaris began her research in February 2020, the saber had just been "returned" to Senegal by Édouard Philippe. At the Army Museum, it was said that the object would not come back, even if, officially, it was only for storage. The first step had been to retrace the saber's entry into the collections—and therefore to locate the letters.

"I had found references to those correspondences, but no information about where they were. So, with some colleagues, we went up to the archives, opened all the crates, and we ended up finding them!"

The image brought a smile to my face. This was how stories began: you opened one crate, then another, then yet another.

The following step had been to verify the origin that Archinard had indicated: the siege of Bandiagara, April 29, 1893. To do that, Lucile Paraponaris had spent several weeks in the National Overseas Archives in Aix-en-Provence, then had examined the documents from the Fréjus archives, and consulted the French Defense Historical Service. I smiled again. We had followed the same path, but in the opposite direction. I had left from Ségou in 1890, and she had begun in 1909 and gone back in time.

"All I have right now about that saber are hypotheses, nothing is certain," she said.

After all those months of research, that letter from Archinard that I had consulted the previous day remained the only written proof that she had found any connection between the saber and El Hadj Oumar Tall.

"Archinard had presented it as such, and we had entered it into the inventory as such. But when we looked a little more carefully into the story, we realized we had nothing else."

Lucile Paraponaris had consulted the military documents kept in France that had to do with the siege of Bandiagara. She found no trace of the saber there. She specifically noted that that had surprised her, because Archinard was often very precise in his descriptions. Why would he have failed to mention a saber of such importance?

"I also found it odd that he knew who the saber belonged to. El Hadj Oumar had been dead for about thirty years. Besides, Bandiagara was abandoned when Archinard entered the town with his troops, and Ahmadou had left a few days before that. So, where had he gotten that information?"

For a while, she wondered whether Archinard had been mistaken, if he had actually kept the saber from Ségou with him so he could donate it to the Army Museum with an invented origin. For my part, I wondered why Archinard would have changed the origin like that, while, in the same letter he listed other objects taken at Ségou. Unless he had knowingly wanted to construct the full narrative of each of his victories through the objects. Unless he desperately needed an object from Bandiagara to complete his list. Perhaps. But Lucile Paraponaris arrived at the same conclusion as I did: the description of the saber from Ségou on exhibit in 1893 did not correspond to the weapon donated by Archinard sixteen years later.

"I do not think that saber is linked to Ségou," she concluded. "And I don't think it was connected to El Hadj Oumar either. I think it was connected to one of his sons. Ahmadou, maybe, or Aguibou. We know that the latter had given several gifts to Archinard."

She had also wondered how that weapon originating from France, with its blade manufactured by Klingenthal, had ended up with the Toucouleur, and was subsequently altered with an African-made handle.

"Once again, all I have are hypotheses. It could be a gift from the French, just as it could be a weapon that was picked up from a battlefield by a Toucouleur warrior."

A spoil of war turned gift, a gift that ended up being a spoil of war, a gift that was altered and regifted. The hypotheses were peppered with doubts and uncertainties, and examining the archives did not manage to clear them up. One thing was certain: Archinard was the only one who referred to the saber as belonging to El Hadj Oumar Tall. There were no other sources.

Later, during one final trip to Senegal, I returned to the National Archives in Dakar to be sure. I went through the military documents relating to the siege of Bandiagara that were kept there. And I found no trace of any saber.

In his daily reports, Archinard alluded to old books that had been found in Bandiagara. In his military report, he mentioned letters from Ahmadou found in the latter's tata. In his marching journal, the search of the tata ordered by Archinard was well documented, as were his findings: "All that remain are a few pieces of silver jewelry, obviously forgotten, some earthenware, kitchen utensils, a Winchester rifle, and other items, most of them worthless."

The most valuable seizure seemed to be a group of two hundred women, distributed as wives to the troops' riflemen. No trace of any saber.

But here was the thing: while Lucile Paraponaris was carrying out her research on the saber, while she was noticing the uncertainties accumulating and the hypotheses multiplying, a legislative procedure was underway. In July 2020, a bill "concerning the restitution of cultural property to the Republic of Benin and to the Republic of Senegal" was filed at the French National Assembly. The law would permit the return of twenty-six objects, at the time part of the collections of the Quai Branly Museum, to be returned to Benin, which included the statues of kings Béhanzin, Glélé and Ghézo—the human-sized statues that sat imposingly in that museum's Africa Room. The saber attributed to El Hadj Oumar—the one in the Army Museum's collections—was also in that bill. On July 26, 2019, the Republic of Senegal made an official request for restitution, the text indicated.

The story of the objects from Benin was very different from that of the saber. Their origin was documented meticulously; there was no doubt about their status as spoils of war. As the parliamentary discussions were taking place between July and December 2020, Lucile Paraponaris was wrapping up her research and following the debates. Little was said about the saber. The objects from Benin took center stage.

All the same, at the Senate hearing Catherine Morin-Desailly, who drafted the law, posed the question to the Minister of Culture, Roselyne Bachelot.

"According to scientific research, the saber that was returned to Senegal never belonged to El Hadj Oumar Tall. That said, what is its symbolic meaning? Whereas the bill clearly lays the foundation for other texts to come, isn't it problematic to return an object that does not quite correspond to the authenticity of the approach?

The Ministry of Culture and the Army Museum have never hidden the fact that the history of the saber was never entirely certain, that it was shrouded in mystery," the Minister replied. "That not only shows the care that is needed to research its origin, but also the difficulty that oral traditions sometimes pose, which are not always easy to preserve, not to mention the absence of sources. Regardless of that, that saber was given to the Army Museum by Louis Archinard, a member of the French armed forces who participated in military campaigns in West Africa at the end of the 19th century. There is no question that it came from El Hadj Oumar Tall's family—a number of elements attest to that fact— probably from his son, the founder of the Toucouleur Empire, whose memory is still very much alive in Senegal today. The official restitution of that object to Senegal is a strong symbolic gesture made by France so that the saber can remain on display for the public in Dakar."

Lucile Paraponaris had followed the debates and was shocked.

"We were part of that law, but it is as if the saber had not counted," she explained. "Certainly, there were political and diplomatic reasons. After all, we are a museum that depends on the Minister of the Armies. But then, why act as if research mattered? The research of origins is a discipline that is currently developing, and here we are denying it. It is counterproductive. If there must be restitution, we need to listen to the research."

She thought back to Emmanuel Macron's speech during the restitution ceremony of the twenty-six objects from Benin on October 27, 2021, at Quai Branly. The president had insisted on the importance of expertise.

"We need to develop the research of origins, better document the circumstances of one work or another when it enters French collections, and crosscheck several expert opinions case by case."

Confronted with those words, Lucile Paraponaris wondered again what purpose all those many months of that research she had carried out for so many months had served.

ACTION OR TRUTH?

PARIS, FRANCE, QUAI BRANLY MUSEUM

Almost three years after my first visit to the archives of the Quai Branly Museum, I went back on the trail of the jewelry from Ségou. I walked along the footbridge above the museum gardens which connected the administrative building to that which housed the exhibition platforms. Lise Mész welcomed me into her office where a large window opened onto the Seine, like a tableau vivant of Paris. On the heritage curator's computer, a special folder contained all the archival documents that she and her colleagues from the Army Museum, the Museum of Natural History in Le Havre and the National Library of France had been able to gather on Archinard's collection, in particular on the siege of Ségou.

"Our goal is to establish a source guide that European and African researchers who are interested in these objects can use," Lise Mész explained. "I would like Senegalese and Malian colleagues to join this working group too, to compare colonial sources in France with colonial sources in Africa as well as the countries' oral traditions."

The curator had held the position of advisor on the history of collections for a little over a year—a position that had been created by the museum's president, Emmanuel Kasarhérou, called to head the institution in 2020.

Lise Mész's work was to coordinate the origin research of the collections. The task was enormous: there were three hundred eighty thousand works in all and the curator did not have a designated team. So, emphasis was placed on the objects for which there was some urgency—in other words on those that had received restitution requests.

"Currently, we have requests from seven different African States," Lise Mész explained. "Half of them are about specific objects; the other half are about the entire collection from the country in question. Those requests are based on the Sarr-Savoy report and the premise that the dissymmetry of the power relationship during the colonial period leaves a right to restitution to African countries today."

The report in question, ordered by President Emmanuel Macron, and published in 2018, indeed advocated for their return. The problem was that it in no case constituted a doctrine of the French State, contrary to what its commander may have conveyed. For restitution to happen, you had to legislate each time.

"It's the circumstances in which they were acquired and origin studies that are going to provide the arguments to propose a bill to the council of ministers," the curator explained. "We are in a very complex legal process that mobilizes the entire parliamentary apparatus, which is triggered on a case-by-case basis."

Thus, the importance of the studies Lise Mész coordinated. She insisted on sharing knowledge and pooling resources with her African colleagues.

"In that research, we try to do things together, to have a diversity of voices."

That is how the museum had come to host the director of the National Museum of Chad for three months for a joint project on the collections and was preparing to receive the director of the National Museum of Mali for a similar visit.

Regarding the jewelry from the Treasure of Ségou, a first step in laying the groundwork had been taken in the archives in France, "thanks to a doctoral student who was able to work on the topic for three months," Lise Mész acknowledged.

Out of the ninety-six pieces of gold and silver jewelry selected for the ad hoc committee established in Kayes in April 1890, there were only twenty-two pieces remaining in the Quai Branly reserves. Between the thefts of 1914 and 1937, the objects that were either lost or missing inventory numbers, that was all that remained of the treasure Archinard had dreamed up to justify the urgency of the siege of Ségou to his superiors.

The same held true at the Army Museum where more than half of the objects could not be located in the reserves. Here too, some of the jewelry remained untraceable, probably because of a lost label or an incorrectly assigned inventory number.

"Very recently, we found one of the pieces of jewelry like that," Lise Mész told me. "It had been numbered incorrectly. Obviously, we are not proud of having lost track of it but you have to admit: that's an issue that arises in all museums."

The next step, on the remaining small corpus, would focus on the materials, alloys and techniques that were used. I thought of Makhtar Niang, the jewelry maker in Saint-Louis, and what he had said to me when I had shown him the photos of the jewelry that I had dug up in the Quai Branly archives: "They should ask for help from the jewelers from here. We know that jewelry. We're knowledgeable about it. We know how to restore it and take care of it." Despite the willingness the curator exhibited, collaborations with African artisans were still mere intentions.

Paradoxically, the debate that President Emmanuel Macron's statement in 2017 sparked seemed to have had more concrete consequences outside of France. At the beginning of 2022, Belgium gave back a complete inventory of around eighty-four thousand objects to the Democratic Republic of Congo which were then part of the collections of the Tervuren Museum, for more transparency. In the United Kingdom, where national institutions such as the British Museum refused any kind of restitution, private museums like Scotland's University of Aberdeen Museum committed to restitution in 2021.

The Netherlands adopted a demanding resolution, "recognizing the injustice done to local populations of former colonial territories when cultural objects had been taken against their will." The "Pressing Matter" project, led by nine museums and the free university of Amsterdam, with a budget of 4.5 million euros, aimed to provide museums with practical advice on their colonial collections.

More spectacularly, Germany signed an agreement with the State of Nigeria on the return of several hundreds of works from the royal palace of Edo (today Benin City). Some pieces would stay in Germany, but only in the form of a loan, the property being transferred to Nigeria. Germany invested in origin research in 2019 by creating a specific fund focused on the colonial period, which has financed forty projects for a total budget of 4.4 million euros.

Those figures are completely disproportionate to the means available to French cultural institutions for carrying out that same kind of research today. If positions have been created, such as those of Lise Mész at the Quai Branly Museum or Lucile Paraponaris at the Army Museum, we are nowhere close to the amount of money invested elsewhere. However, that research is essential if we want restitution to be based on scientific findings.

"The methods of acquisition must be specified every time," Lise Mész noted. "Is it spoils of war, a confiscation by the colonial administration, an object resulting from trafficking or illicit searches, taken in a power struggle, or simply a purchase? The art market was growing a lot, and there were objects produced for European taste, which never had any other use. There is confusion about whether all African collections were the result of colonial plunder. It is more complex than that."

"Isn't that understandable backlash?" I asked. "Since so little has been told in European museums about the origin of objects and their history? We are asked to have a simple aesthetic view."

"It is true that there is no discussion about colonial history," Lise replied. "We need to think about how to talk about those collections with a plurality of voices, displaying all their complexity. And to have those conversations, we need transparency. With a real cooperation among scholars in Africa and in Europe."

Perhaps it was precisely history passed on silently that left so much room for ideology and symbolism. I thought again of the "saber said to belong to El Hadj Oumar" and its restitution which I now know took place despite it being impossible to demonstrate a connection between the object and the historical figure. Was it necessary then not to return the object, even though during those former trips to Senegal it had acquired the status that then justified the request for return? Which of those truths mattered most: that of the archives or that of the symbol?

On the day of the restitution ceremony in Dakar, everyone agreed that it was the gesture of the return that was what should take precedence—who cared if whether the particular object was perhaps not the one that best filled the criteria that origin research was trying to develop? Maybe, I said to myself as I walked out of the office, maybe that choice is also what preserves each individual's freedom to tell his or her own version of the story, without worrying about the other's version. And perhaps that was what allowed us to claim the truth is on my side.

Before I left the museum, I walked through the Africa Hall again. The Shark—Man was no longer there, nor was the Bird—Man or the Lion—Man. The palace doors had disappeared, and so had the throne. After one last temporary farewell exhibition, the twenty-six objects from the Royal Palace of Abomey—twenty-six out of three thousand one hundred fifty-seven works originating from that country—were back on the road to Benin to be placed on display in Cotonou, as they awaited the opening of a new museum. In their place, in that room, was a giant Ijele mask made of cloth and wood, three meters high, designed for the exhibition titled "The Magicians of the Earth" in 1989 by Nigerian artist Mike Chukwukelu. It was as though we had suddenly traveled from one era into another, from the venerated art objects of a royal palace to the work of a new contemporary artist.

EPILOGUE

This book is a work of nonfiction written based on historical documents and interviews. It is the fruit of the work of an author, not an historian, and does not lay claim to a comprehensive established or historical truth. I have applied the same principles that govern my work when I put on my journalist's hat: a single source is not sufficient. You have to cross-reference. But there are always sources that elude us, voices that could have been heard but were non't.

When it came time to finish this story, I thought about all the blind spots in my investigation.

I wanted to see Caliph Thierno Madani Tall again so I could give him photos of Abdoulaye's letters, but I ended up giving my USB drive to his assistant, Ibrahima Sy. I wanted to travel to Mali, to the places where an important part of this story took place—to Kayes, to Ségou, and to Bandiagara. For three years, I hoped that the insecurity that persists in the region would dissipate, that the jihadist threat would go away. That is not what happened. The irony of history is that the end of this story, which begins with a holy war, is prevented from being told because of another holy war, although of a different nature and in a much more complex context. Therefore, I will not go to Abdoulaye's tomb in Ségou. I will not look for the statue of Archinard, which, it seems, is still conserved there. I will not visit Kayes from where the cases of jewelry and manuscripts departed. Nor will I go to Bandiagara where El Hadj Oumar Tall allegedly died and where Archinard allegedly found a saber that had belonged to him. I will not hear what Malians have to say about this story—Malians who have never demanded that those objects be returned, who are the heirs to the kingdoms attacked by El Hadj Oumar, then by his son Ahmadou, and whose heritage in part was pillaged or destroyed by the former.

My story ends there, in the Africa Hall of the Quai Branly Museum, in the empty space left by the Shark—Man, now filled by the work of an artist who is still living. In a few months, when this book comes out, next to objects from another royal palace, the Oba Palace in Nigeria, there will be a panel which will tell about war, pillage, and looting—a text which will finally bring voice to the violence of that journey for all to see. So, something will have changed.

ACKNOWLEDGMENTS

This book would not have been possible without the gracious assistance of all those who accepted to meet me, to answer my questions and patiently enlighten my ignorance.

I offer my warm thanks to:

Caliph Thierno Madani Tall,
    as well as his assistant Ibrahima Sy in Dakar,
    and Thierno Mahmoud Tall and Oumar Tall in Halwar

In Dakar:
    Hamady Bocoum
    Felwine Sarr
    Abdoulaye Sokhna Diop

In Saint-Louis:
    Makhtar Niang
    Arête Sarr Mbodj, as well as the entire team at Lycée El Hadj Oumar Foutiyou Tall

In Podor:
- Abdourahmane Niang
- Ibrahima Sy

In Le Havre:
- Gabrielle Baglione
- Cédric Crémière
- Anne Liénard
- Mamadou Ly
- Claude Malon
- Thierry Vincent

In Paris:
- Lise Mész
- Lucile Paraponaris

Thanks to all those who made the following meetings possible:
- Jarmo Pikkujämsä, in Saint-Louis
- Nadjirou Sall, in Podor
- Saliou Guèye, in Dakar

Finally, and especially:

To Mamadou Samba Mbow and Ndiabou Séga Touré, who have followed this story from the beginning, who have shared *atayas*, *soupoukandjas* and debates with me, one word: *a jaraama*.

For their help and sound advice, my thanks to the archivists at the National Archives of Senegal in Dakar, at the Center for Research and Documentation in Saint-Louis, at the Army Museum and the Quai Branly Museum in Paris, at the National Overseas Archives in Aix-en-Provence, at the Center for the Historical Study of Overseas Troops in Fréjus and at the municipal archives in Le Havre.

Thanks to the youth at Alter Natives, to Emmanuelle Cadet and Issa Dia, who showed me around the archives and taught me to sharpen my perspective on history. Zoul, Marie and Diariétou, Ahmed, Manthia and Marilou, Imane, Oussam and Aminatou, Demba, Bamba and all the others, the past belongs to you, the storytellers of tomorrow.

To my editors, Cyril Gay and Clémence Billault, thank you for this second book journey.

And lastly, I am eternally grateful to my tribe whose love and indulgence accompanies each story I tell.

BRIEF SELECTIVE BIBLIOGRAPHY

Some publications have been particularly helpful to me throughout this investigation:

Cuttier, Martine. *Portrait du colonialism triumphant: Louis Archinard (1850-1932)* [A Portrait of Triumphant Colonialism: Louis Archinard (1850-1932)], Lavauzelle, 2006.

Dieng, Samba. *La Geste d'El Hadj Oumar et l'islamisation de l'épopée peule* [El Hadj Oumar's Gest and the Islamization of the Fulani Epic], Karthala, 2017.

Foliard, Daniel. "Les vies du 'trésor de Ségou'" [The Many Lives of the Treasure of Ségou] in Revue *historique* (Historical Review), 2018/4, no. 688.

Foliard, Daniel. *Combattre, punir, photographier. Empires coloniaux, 1890-1914*. [Fight, Punish, Photograph: Colonial Empires, 1890-1914] La Découverte, 2020.

Malon, Claude. *Le Havre colonial de 1880 à 1960*. [Colonial Le Havre from 1880 to 1960] Presses universitaires de Caen, 2006.

Malon, Claude. *Le Promeneur des non-lieux*. Éditions des Falaises, 2020.

Oluruntimehin, B.O. *The Ségou Tukulor Empire*. Longman, 1972.

Sarr, Felwine and Bénédicte Savoy. *Restituer le patrimoine africain*. Philippe Rey/Le Seuil, 2018.

Bénédicte Savoy's lectures at the Collège de France, between 2016 and 2020, helped me to understand the cultural history of heritage and the issues that arise when objets d'art circulate.

AUTHOR AND TRANSLATOR BIOS

Born in Finland in 1973, **TAINA TERVONEN** is a French-Finnish journalist, filmmaker and author writing in in French and Finnish and currently based in Paris. Self-described as a "teller of true stories," she is the author of several books of non-fiction that deal with serious social topics. Her work, *The Country of the Disappeared*, was the winner of the 2019 Louise Weiss Prize for European Journalism, and her film *Talking with the Dead* was selected of the Cinéma du Réel festival in 2020. She is the recipient for the Jan Michalski Award (https://fondation-janmichalski.com/en/prix) in 2022 for *The Bone Whisperers*, originally published as "Les Fossoyeuses" (Editions Marchialy) in 2021.

SARA HANABURGH is a scholar (French and Francophone African literature and cinema) and translator working between French, Portuguese, Spanish and English. Her literary translations include *Kaveena* by Boubacar Boris Diop (*Kaveena*, 2016), co-translated with Bhakti Shringarpure, and Angèle Rawiri's novel Fureurs et cris de femmes (*The Fury and Cries of Women*, 2014). Her articles and translations have appeared in africaisacountry.com, *The Savannah Review*, Warscapes, The Dictionary of African Biography, Imagine Africa, v. 3 and C& América Latina. She teaches at St. John's University and is currently editing a volume on the history of adaptation of African literature to the screen. She was the translator for *The Stonebreakers* by Emmanuel Dongala, published in 2023 by Schaffner Press. She lives in New York.